# Multicultural Crafts from Recycled Materials

## from the Choose to Reuse Series

**Written by Deborah Whitacre and Becky Radtke**

**Illustrated by Becky Radtke**

Teaching & Learning Company

1204 Buchanan St., P.O. Box 10

Carthage, IL 62321

## This book belongs to

______________________________

This book is dedicated to my wonderful husband, John.—Deborah

This is for my sister, Debbie.—Becky

We would like to thank Bubs Kennedy, our teacher consultant, for the valuable contributions she made to this book.

This book was developed for the Teaching & Learning Company by The Good Neighbor Press, Inc., Grand Junction, CO.

Cover photo by Images and More Photography



ISBN No. 1-57310-025-0

Printing No. 98765432

**Teaching & Learning Company**
**1204 Buchanan St., P.O. Box 10**
**Carthage, IL 62321**

# Table of Contents


**The Arctic**
- Super Scrimshaw Necklace . . . . . . . . . . . . 1

**Africa**
- African Basket Pencil Holder . . . . . . . . . . . 3
- Brilliant Beads . . . . . . . . . . . . . . . . . . . . . . . 5
- Delightful African Drum . . . . . . . . . . . . . . . 7
- Happy Hippo Magnet . . . . . . . . . . . . . . . . . 9
- Simple Sotho Doll . . . . . . . . . . . . . . . . . . . 12

**Brazil**
- Brimmed Brazilian Hat . . . . . . . . . . . . . . . 15

**Central America**
- Whimsical Worry Doll . . . . . . . . . . . . . . . 17

**China**
- Fun Foam Prints . . . . . . . . . . . . . . . . . . . . 19
- New Year's Dragon Puppet . . . . . . . . . . . . 21
- Tricky Tangram Picture . . . . . . . . . . . . . . . 24

**Colombia**
- Straw on the String Game . . . . . . . . . . . . 27

**Guatemala**
- Cascading Cascarones . . . . . . . . . . . . . . . 29

**India**
- Dipas Raft . . . . . . . . . . . . . . . . . . . . . . . . . 31

**Italy**
- Behold Our Beautiful Buttons . . . . . . . . . 33

**Japan**
- "Fan"tastic Japanese Fan . . . . . . . . . . . . . . 36
- Rice Field-Worker . . . . . . . . . . . . . . . . . . 40

**Korea**
- Cinch Ch̆omsŏngdale Observatory . . . . . 43

**Mexico**
- Colorful Castanets . . . . . . . . . . . . . . . . . . 46
- Gorgeous God's Eye . . . . . . . . . . . . . . . . . 49
- Lovely Lid Mosaic . . . . . . . . . . . . . . . . . . . 51
- Magnificent Mexican Poncho . . . . . . . . . . 53
- Musical Maracas . . . . . . . . . . . . . . . . . . . . 55
- Pretty Pottery . . . . . . . . . . . . . . . . . . . . . . 57

**Native Americans**
- Cute Cradleboard . . . . . . . . . . . . . . . . . . . 60
- Mini Hide Tanner . . . . . . . . . . . . . . . . . . . 63
- Mysterious Mask . . . . . . . . . . . . . . . . . . . . 66
- Terrific Tepee . . . . . . . . . . . . . . . . . . . . . . 69
- Totally Awesome Totem Pole . . . . . . . . . . 71

**Reproducibles**
- Save 'n' Send/Sufficiently Stocked . . . . . . 74
- Certificate . . . . . . . . . . . . . . . . . . . . . . . . . 75

**Resources** . . . . . . . . . . . . . . . . . . . . . . . . . 76


The crafts pictured on the front cover are the Delightful African Drum (page 7), the New Year's Dragon Puppet (page 21) and the Totally Awesome Totem Pole (page 71).

# Dear Teacher or Parent,

Recycling is on everyone's minds these days. We are all trying hard to pull together to protect and preserve the Earth for future generations. This book offers you the unique opportunity to involve your students in this effort. It is our hope that your students will discover how they, too, can be an important part of saving their planet. What better way to show them the benefits of choosing to reuse than by creating these fun craft projects?

The crafts in this book all use items that the average household often throws away. (You'll notice that throughout this book an asterisk has been placed by each item that is being recycled.) The easy-to-follow instructions will help you to guide your students in turning recyclable items into marvelous multicultural crafts. For safety reasons, we advise you to closely supervise your students while they make the crafts in this book. Use your good judgement and consider the child's age and abilities to modify certain steps or processes when you feel it is necessary. Always carefully read and follow the directions and warnings given on the materials you use. Each craft comes illustrated and (if necessary) with reproducible patterns. All of these crafts can be used to help children learn about other cultures of the world.

At the back of this book you will find a fun, reproducible certificate. For your convenience, we have also included reproducible letters to parents and guardians requesting that they please send or stop sending household recyclable items.

As the owner of this book, you are entitled and welcomed to use all the art contained for classroom purposes (wall and door decorations, bulletin board designs, flyers, invitations, etc.). We hope that this book will be used and enjoyed by you over and over again during your teaching career.

Sincerely,

Becky & Deborah

Deborah Whitacre

Becky Radtke

# Super Scrimshaw Necklace

## ■ Perfect Timing

Make this multicultural craft when studying the Arctic or reading:

- *Nessa's Fish.* Nancy Luenn. Atheneum Publishers, 1990.
- *Very Last First Time.* Jan Andrews. Atheneum Publishers, 1986.
- *Mama, Do You Love Me?* Barbara M. Joosse. Scholastic Inc., 1991.

## ■ Materials Needed

- white Styrofoam™ tray* (students can share one)
- brown washable marker
- crayon
- pencil
- paper towel
- 30" (76.2 cm) piece of yarn
- paper punch

## ■ Tell the Class

"Lots of Inuit people enjoy carving things. It's a skill that takes a lot of patience and practice. A scrimshaw is a kind of carving that is made from a whalebone or piece of ivory.

It would be pretty hard to find whalebone or ivory around here, so we're going to use something else to make a necklace. When we're finished, it will be similar to what the Inuit make."

## ■ How to Make It

**For Teachers, Aides and Parent Volunteers**

**A.** Photocopy an oval pattern for each student.

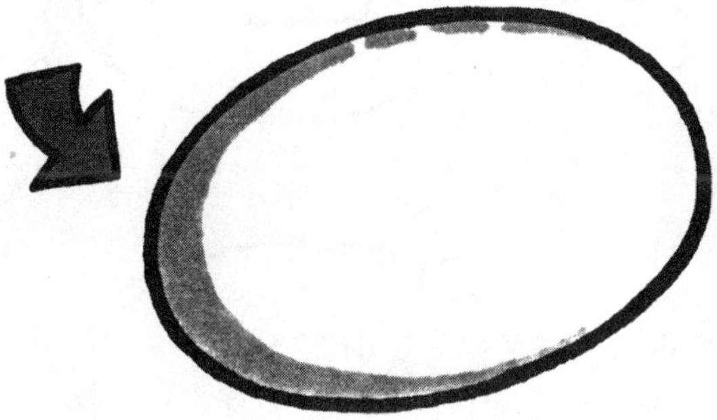

**B.** Cut 30" (76.2 cm) pieces of yarn. Every student will need one piece.

## How to Make It

**For Students**

1. Cut the oval pattern out. Then use a crayon to trace around it onto the Styrofoam™ tray. Cut it out. (You can get five oval pieces from one tray, so share with classmates.)

2. Use a pencil and press down firmly to draw a half circle in the middle of the oval. Then add an eye and tail to make a whale (as shown here).

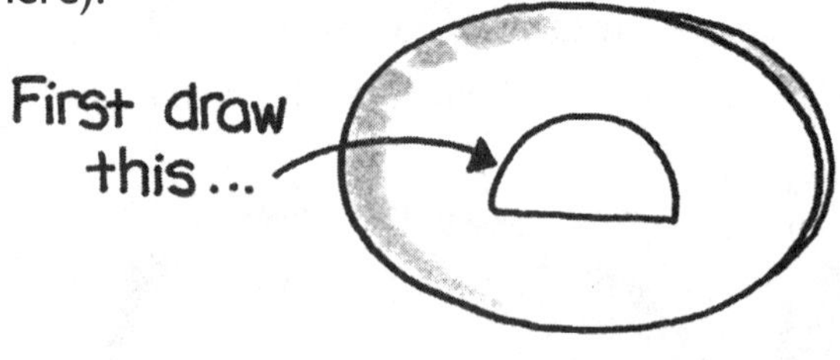

3. Paper-punch a hole above the whale.

4. Use a brown washable marker to completely color the oval. Let it dry for one minute. Then take a paper towel and wipe off the oval. This should darken the lines. Let it dry a little while.

5. String a piece of yarn through the paper-punched hole and knot the ends. Wear your necklace at home and tell your family how you made it.

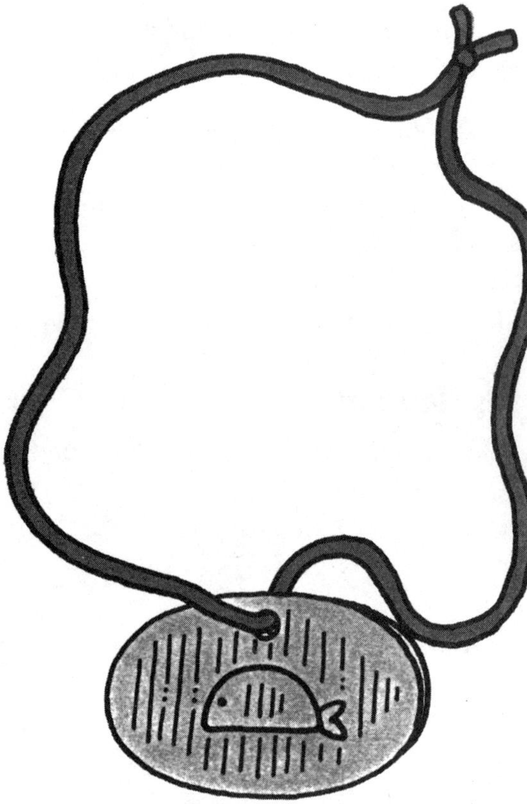

# African Basket Pencil Holder

## Perfect Timing

Make this multicultural craft when studying the continent and people of Africa or reading:

- *Bringing the Rain to Kapiti Plain.* Verna Aardema. Dial Books, 1981.
- *Why Mosquitoes Buzz in People's Ears: A West African Tale.* Verna Aardema. Dial Books, 1975.
- *Song of the Boat.* Lorenz Graham. Crowell, 1975.

## Materials Needed

- frozen juice can (12 oz. [354.9 ml] size)*
- white paper strip
- tightly woven smooth basket
- brown crayon
- brown yarn
- glue
- scissors

## Tell the Class

If possible, bring several handwoven smooth baskets to the class that children can share to make this craft.

"African people are admired for their basket weaving skills. They use baskets to carry many different things. Sometimes they balance them on their heads as they walk.

Let's make a pencil holder that looks like a basket. You can keep it for yourself or give it as a gift!"

## How to Make It

**For Teachers, Aides and Parent Volunteers**

**A.** Cut white paper (photocopy paper is fine) into 9" x 4¾" (22.86 x 12.07 cm) strips. Each student will need one.

**B.** Cut brown yarn into 11" (27.94 cm) pieces. Each student will need one piece.

## How to Make It

**For Students**

1. Lay the white paper strip over a section of the basket.

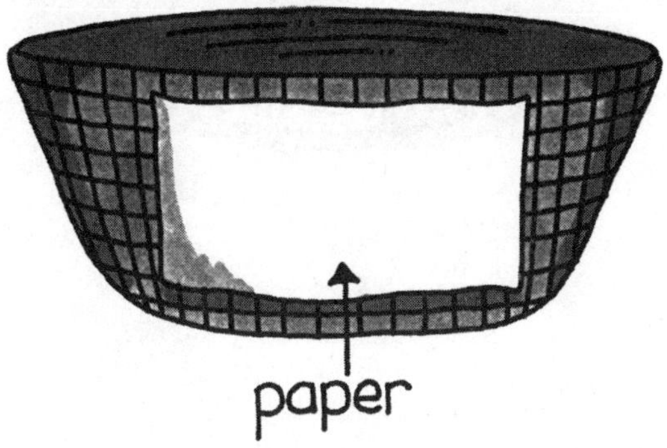

2. Peel the paper off the brown crayon. Using the side, rub it firmly onto the white paper strip. Do the entire strip in this manner. This is an easy way to produce an authentic "woven" look.

3. Glue the finished strip around the juice can.

4. Tie four knots in the brown piece of yarn. Space them as evenly apart as you can.

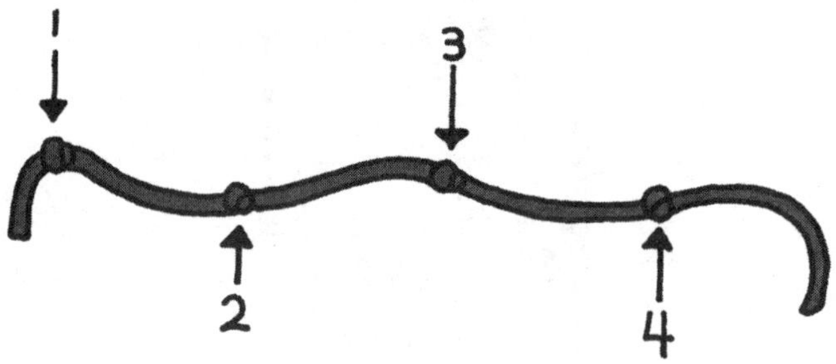


5. Glue the knotted yarn piece around the top of the juice can (about ¼" [.64 cm] from the top).

6. Take your creation home and put pencils in it.

# Brilliant Beads

## Perfect Timing

Make this craft when studying Africa or reading:

- *Africa Dream.* Eloise Greenfield. Crowell, 1977.
- *Darkness and the Butterfly.* Ann Grifalconi. Little, Brown, 1987.
- *Osa's Pride.* Ann Grifalconi. Little, Brown, 1990.

## Materials Needed

- drinking straw (used but rinsed thoroughly)*
- piece of wrapping paper
- yarn
- tape
- glue
- scissors

## Tell the Class

"The African people learned a long time ago how to make beads. They rubbed shells, stones and bones to get holes through them and smooth the edges. Then they would string them onto cords or sew them onto clothing.

We're going to learn a simple way to make some beads. When you've made enough, you can make a necklace with them."

## How to Make It

**For Teachers, Aides and Parent Volunteers**

**A.** Cut the wrapping paper scraps into strips that measure 8" x 2" (20.32 x 5.08 cm).

**B.** Cut the yarn into 34" (86.36 cm) pieces. Cut one for each student.

## How to Make It

**For Students**

1. Spread a thin layer of glue onto the blank side of the piece of wrapping paper.
2. Roll the wrapping paper around the straw and let it dry.

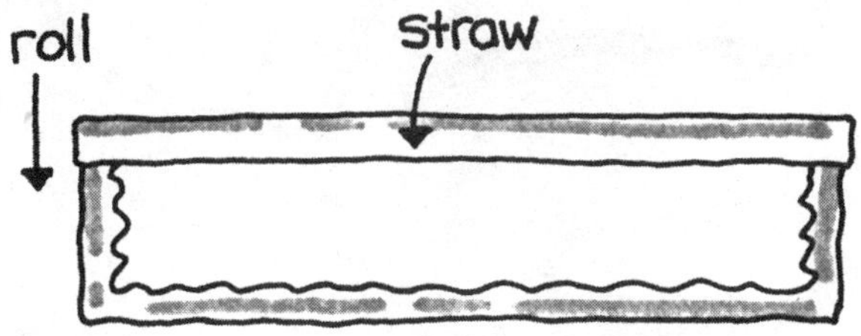


3. Cut the straw into 1" (2.54 cm) pieces. (Younger students will need assistance.)

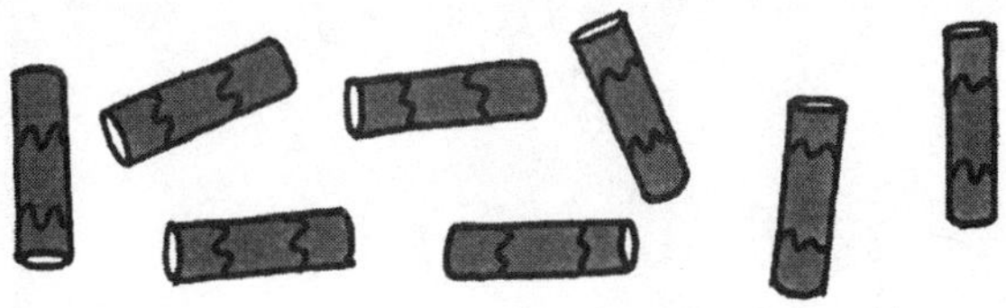

4. If you like, trade beads with other students to obtain a variety.

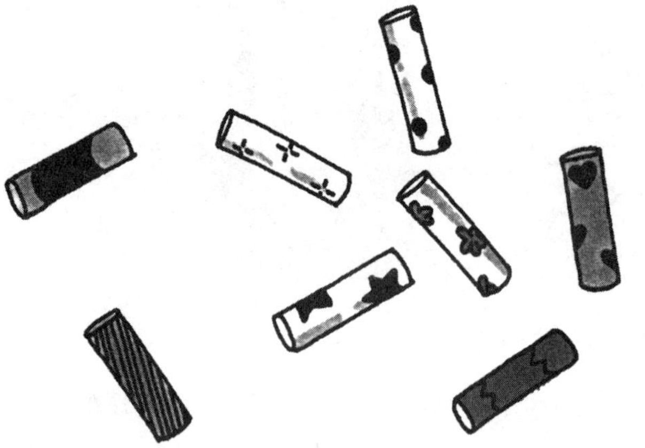

5. Wrap tape around the end of the yarn to act as a "needle."

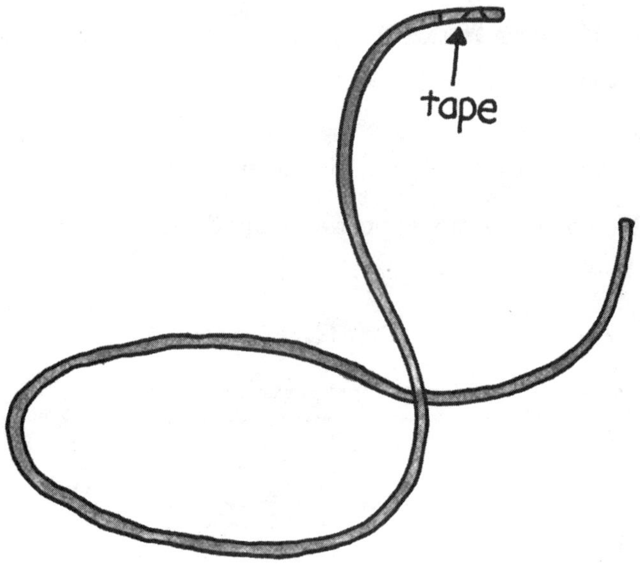


6. Put the beads onto the yarn and knot the ends together to create a necklace.

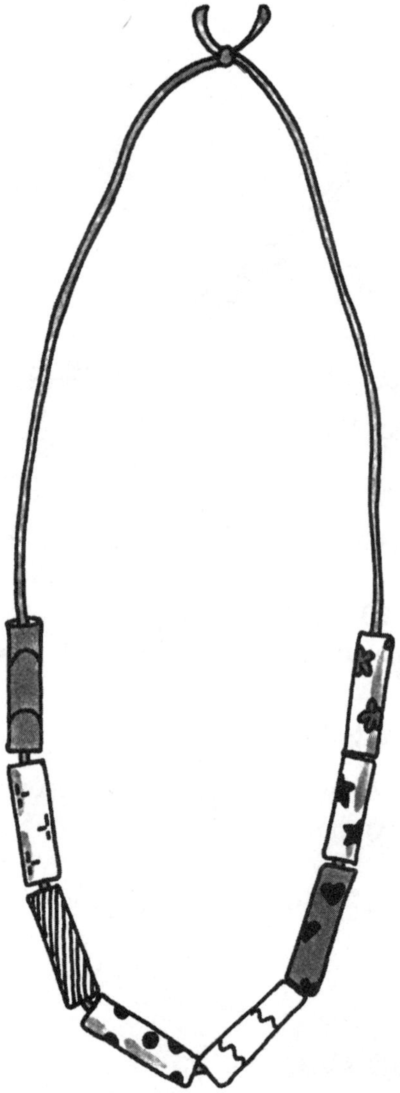

7. Wear your necklace and be proud of what you've made!

# Delightful African Drum

## Perfect Timing

Make this craft when studying Africa or reading:

- *Brother to the Wind.* Mildred Pitts, Walter. Lothrop, Lee & Shepard Books, 1987.
- *Awful Aardvark.* Mwalimu and Adrienne Kennaway. Little, Brown, 1989.
- *Mufaro's Beautiful Daughters: An African Tale.* John Steptoe. Lothrop, Lee & Shepard Books, 1987.

## Materials Needed

- metal coffee can with lid (1lb. 10 oz.)*
- various colors of butcher paper
- various colors of yarn scraps
- pencil
- washable markers
- small lump of clay
- tape
- glue
- scissors

## Tell the Class

"In Africa people play drums with their hands to make music and to send messages to places where there are no telephones. When they do this, each beat of the drum means something. Then the people who are listening use their drums to send a message back.

Let's make our own drums and pretend that we are able to 'talk' back and forth like the Africans do."

## How to Make It

**For Teachers, Aides and Parent Volunteers**

Cut various colors of butcher paper into 2" x 17" (5.08 x 43.18 cm) strips.

## How to Make It

**For Students**

1. Remove the lid and cover the outside of the coffee can by gluing butcher paper strips onto it. Put the lid back on. Tape seams together to make them extra secure.

2. Decorate using markers and scraps of yarn.

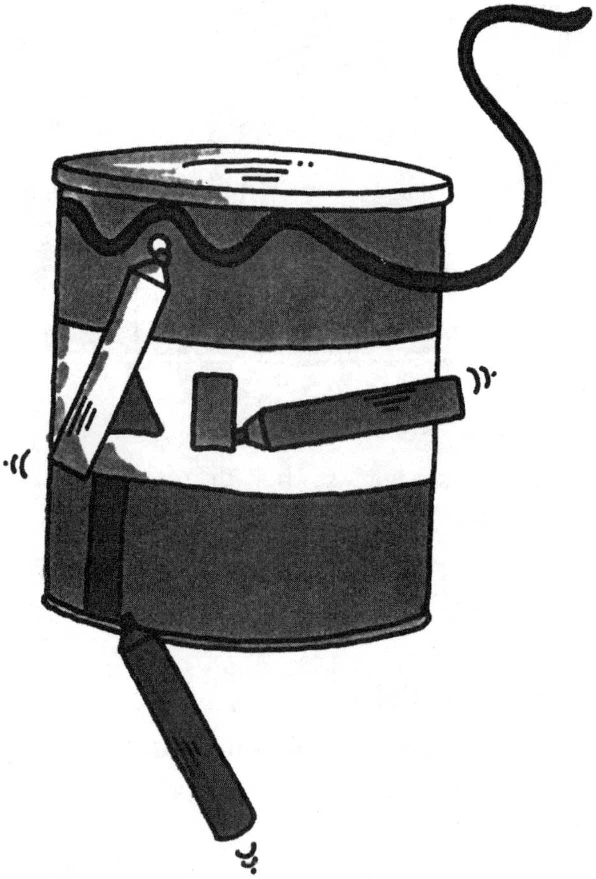

3. Roll the lump of clay into a round ball. Put it onto a pencil as shown to make a drumstick.

4. Use your drumsticks to beat out a pretend message on your drum.

# Happy Hippo Magnet

## Perfect Timing

Make this craft when studying Africa or reading:

- *Princess Gorilla and a New Kind of Water.* Verna Aardema. Dial Books for Young Readers, 1988.
- *The Village of Round and Square Houses.* Ann Grifalconi. Little, Brown, 1986.
- *Who's in Rabbit's House? A Masai Tale.* Verna Aardema. Dial Books for Young Readers, 1982.

## Materials Needed

- juice lid (from a 12 oz. [354.9 ml] can)*
- yellow modeling clay
- red tempera paint
- liquid dishwashing soap (a few drops)
- pencil (with a sharp point)
- magnet strip (You can buy long strips of magnet at craft stores. To help with the cost, you may want to ask for a small amount of money from each child.)
- reproducible "How to Draw a Hippo" (page 11)
- paintbrush
- glue

## Tell the Class

"In Africa there is a soft type of stone called *soapstone.* African people cover this stone with a colored pigment which is like paint. After it dries they use a sharp object to scratch a picture onto it. Many times they draw an animal.

I know of a way that you can make a picture out of modeling clay and make a magnet out of it. Let's get started!"

## How to Make It

### For Teachers, Aides and Parent Volunteers

**A.** Cut magnet strips 1¾" (4.45 cm) long. Every student will need one piece.

**B.** Mix a few drops of liquid dishwashing soap into shallow dishes of red tempera paint. This will help the paint stick to the clay. (Three children can share one dish.)

**C.** Photocopy a sample hippo page for each student.

## How to Make It

### For Students

1. Take a small lump of yellow modeling clay and press it into a juice lid (with the rim up.) Keep working with it until it is one even surface.

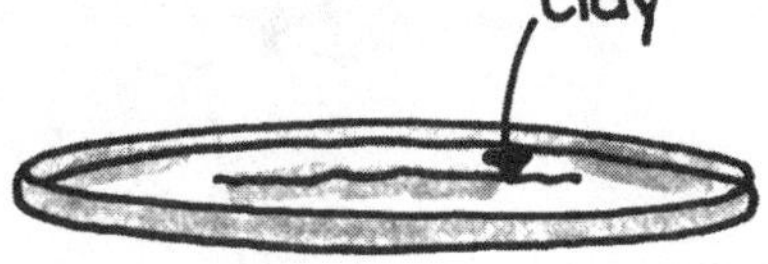

2. Paint the clay with the red tempera paint mixture and let it dry.

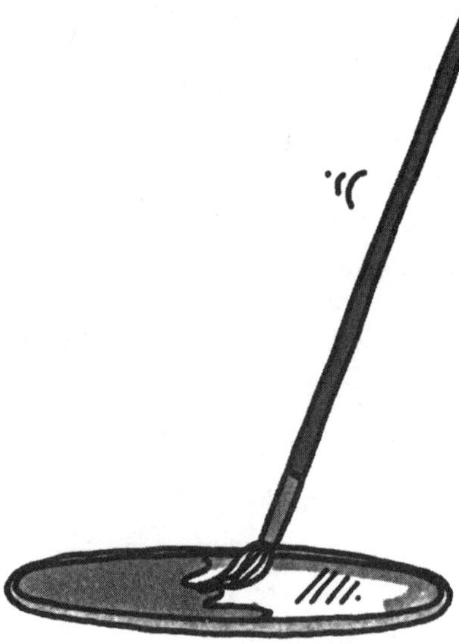

3. Following the instructions on the reproducible page, use a sharp pencil to draw a hippo into the painted modeling clay.

4. Glue the magnet strip onto the back of the lid as shown. Let it dry.

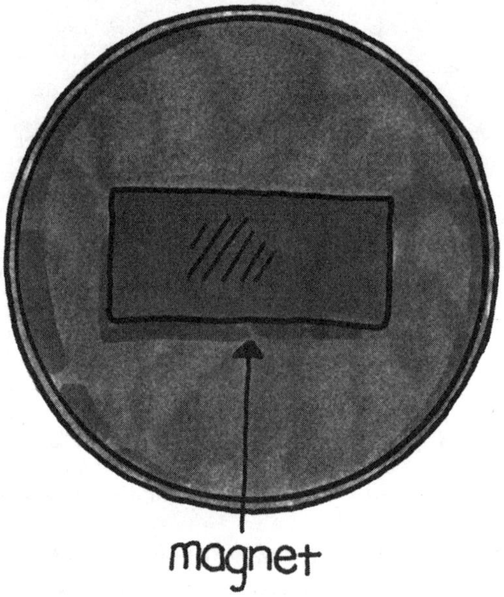


5. Take your hippo magnet home and proudly display it on the refrigerator.

# How to Draw a Hippo

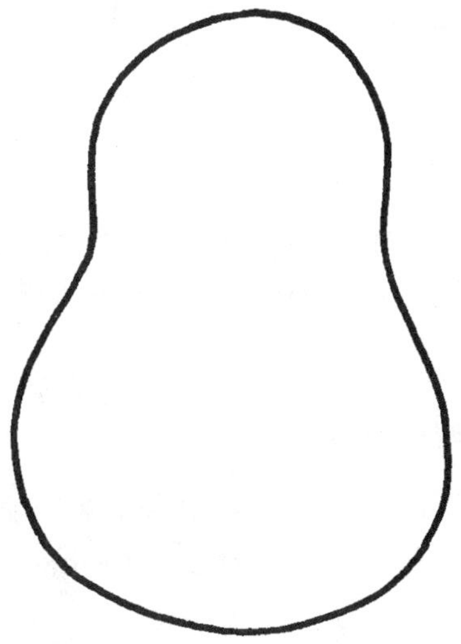

1. Draw a pear shape.

2. Add two small ovals for ears and two dot eyes.

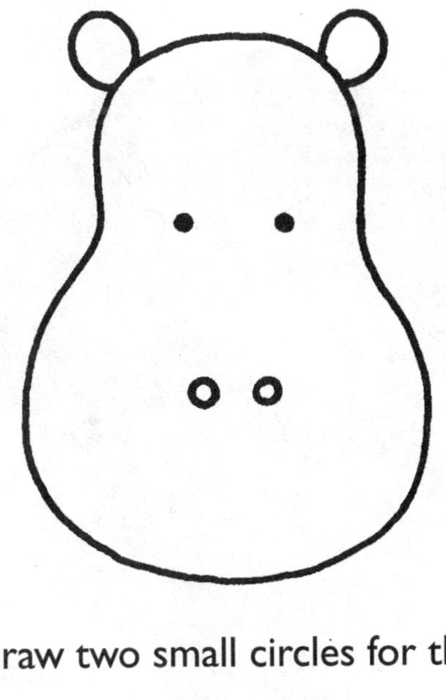

3. Draw two small circles for the nose.

4. Finish by drawing a smiling mouth with two teeth.

# Simple Sotho Doll

## Perfect Timing

Make this craft when studying Africa or reading:

- *The Name of the Tree.* Celia Barker Lottridge. Margaret K. McElderry Books, 1989.
- *How the Guinea Fowl Got Her Spots: A Swahili Tale of Friendship.* Barbara Knutson. Carolrhoda Books, 1990.
- *Flyaway Girl.* Ann Grifalconi. Little, Brown and Co., 1992.

## Materials Needed

- Styrofoam™ cup*
- 2 wire twist ties
- reproducible doll head patterns (page 14)
- crayons or washable markers
- various colors of sequins
- scraps of black yarn
- tape
- glue
- scissors
- pencil

## Tell the Class

"Brides often carry bouquets of flowers at their wedding. In the Sotho community of Africa, brides carry dolls. These dolls have no arms or legs. They wear earrings and are made of beads. They believe the dolls are magic. The African bride names the doll with the name she will give to her firstborn child.

You'll have the chance to make a special doll out of Styrofoam™, and you can name it whatever you want."

## How to Make It

**For Teachers, Aides and Parent Volunteers**

Photocopy the doll head patterns for each student.

## How to Make It

**For Students**

1. Choose a doll head pattern. Color the face and eyes brown and the hair black. Cut it out.
2. With a pencil, poke a small hole through each *X* on each ear. Shape the twist ties around your finger to make circles. Put one through each ear hole to make earrings. (Younger students will need assistance.)

3. Fold the doll head on the dotted lines and tape it to the bottom of the Styrofoam™ cup.

4. Glue sequins onto the cup to make it look beaded.

5. Glue scraps of black yarn onto the hair.

6. Take your Sotho Doll home and put it on your dresser.

# Sotho Doll Head Patterns

# Brimmed Brazilian Hat

## ■ Perfect Timing

Make this craft when studying Brazil or reading *Amazon Boy* by Ted Lewin (Macmillan, 1993).

## ■ Materials Needed

- 9" (22.86 cm) paper plate
- large brown grocery bag*
- brown crayon
- various colored craft feathers
- 2 pieces of yarn
- tape
- scissors

## ■ Tell the Class

"During festivals, children in Brazil like to dress up in special costumes. Part of each costume is a beautiful hat that has been decorated with leaves and feathers.

You're going to have the chance to make a hat that will be something like the ones those children wear."

## ■ How to Make It

**For Teachers, Aides and Parent Volunteers**

Cut 15" (38.1) pieces of yarn. Each student will need two pieces.

## ■ How to Make It

**For Students**

1. Cut the center out of the paper plate. This is what you will place on your head. It is the "brim" of the hat. (For safety reasons, younger students will need assistance.)

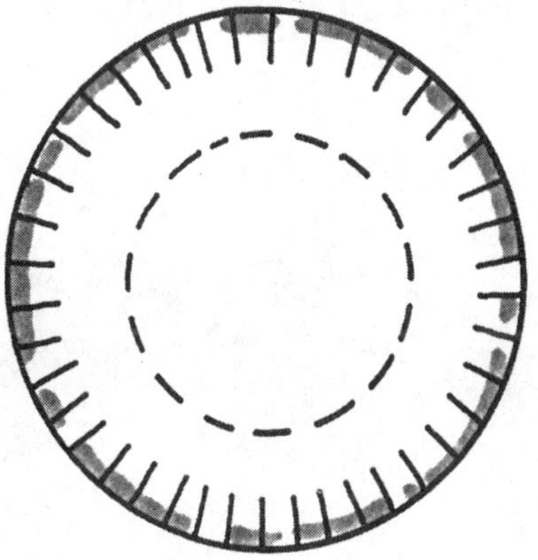

2. Cut leaf shapes out of the brown grocery bag. Use a brown crayon to give the leaves detail.

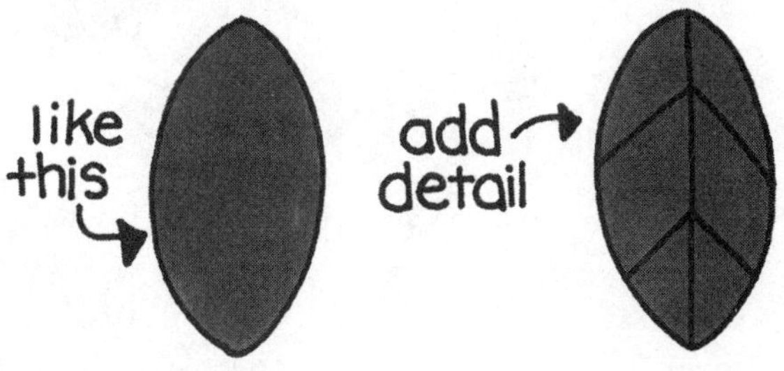

3. Tape the leaves onto the brim allowing some space between each.

4. In the spaces between each leaf, tape a craft feather.

5. Tape the yarn pieces underneath the brim. When you wear the hat, tie these under your chin to keep it secure.

6. Wear your hat at home and show family members.

# Whimsical Worry Doll

## Perfect Timing

Make this craft when studying Central America or reading:

- *Tortillitas Para Mama' and Other Nursery Rhymes.* Margot C. Griego. Holt & Co., 1981.
- *Uncle Nacho's Hat: A Folktale from Nicaragua.* Harriet Rohmer. Childrens Book Press, 1989.
- *The Gold Coin.* A. Ada. Atheneum Publishers, 1991.

## Materials Needed

- 1 craft stick*
- piece of drinking straw
- fine-tip washable markers
- various colors of yarn scraps
- tape
- glue

## Tell the Class

"In Central America they make tiny dolls using wood and yarn. Children are told if they tell this little doll their worries before they go to bed and then place it under their pillow, they will get a restful night of sleep.

Let's make worry dolls of your own!"

## How to Make It

**For Teachers, Aides and Parent Volunteers**

Cut drinking straws into 3" (7.62 cm) pieces. Every student will need one piece.

## How to Make It

**For Students**

Younger students will need assistance with each step except steps 2 and 5.

1. Tape the piece of straw to the craft stick as shown.

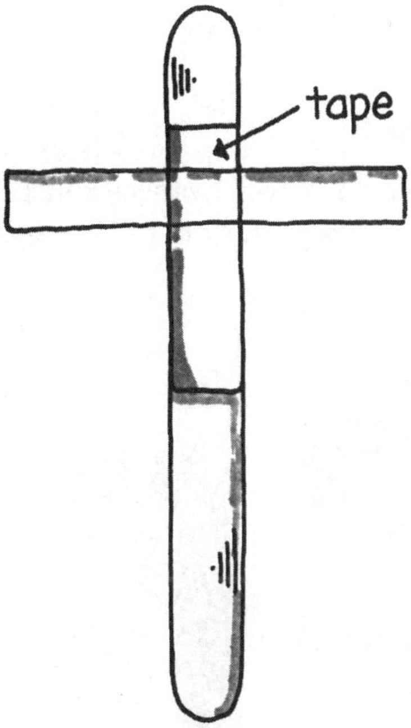


2. Use markers to draw eyes and a mouth.

3. Wrap the doll's arms with various colors of yarn for clothing. Tuck in the loose ends.

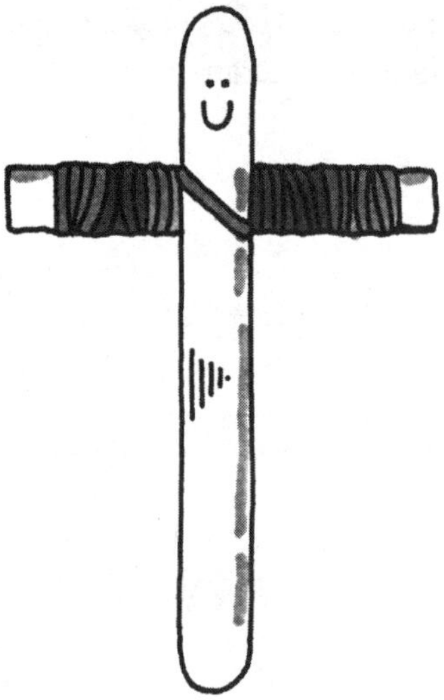

4. Wrap the doll's body with various colors of yarn for clothing. Tuck in the loose ends.

5. Glue a small piece of yarn onto the head for hair.

6. Take your doll home and tell family members how you made it.

# Fun Foam Prints

## Perfect Timing

Make this craft when studying China or reading:

- *The Empty Pot.* Demi. Holt & Co., 1990.
- *The Magic Boat.* Demi. Holt & Co., 1982.
- *Legend of the Milky Way.* Jeanne M. Lee. Holt & Co., 1982.

## Materials Needed

- Styrofoam™ trays* (Each student will need two.)
- variety of tempera paints
- paintbrushes
- reproducible shape patterns
- 3 sheets of white paper for each student
- paper punch
- yarn scraps
- pencil
- scissors
- tape
- glue

## Tell the Class

"Chinese people invented block printing a very long time ago. They carved a symbol into a block of wood, painted it with ink and then pressed it onto a sheet of paper. This is how they made the very first printed books in China.

Let's make some special stampers and do some printing of our own."

## How to Make It

**For Teachers, Aides and Parent Volunteers**

**A.** Go around to each student and cut three 2" x 2" (5.08 x 5.08 cm) squares from one of their Styrofoam™ trays.

**B.** Cut yarn into 4" (10.16 cm) and 6" (15.24 cm) pieces. Each student will need three of each size.

**C.** Photocopy the shape patterns below for each student.

## How to Make It

**For Students**

This craft takes two days to complete. Do steps 1 and 2 the first day.

**1.** Cut out the three photocopied shapes. Trace around them onto the remaining Styrofoam™ tray. Cut them out.

**2.** Glue the Styrofoam™ shapes onto the 2" x 2" (5.08 x 5.08 cm) Styrofoam™ squares as shown. Let them dry overnight.

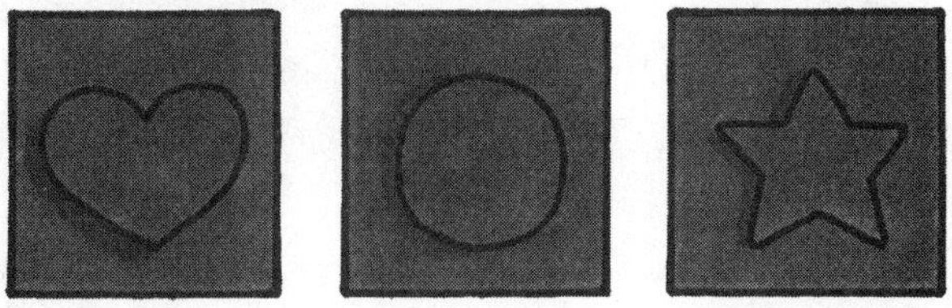

3. The next day tape the 4" (10.16 cm) pieces of yarn to the backs of the stampers as shown. (Younger students will need assistance.)

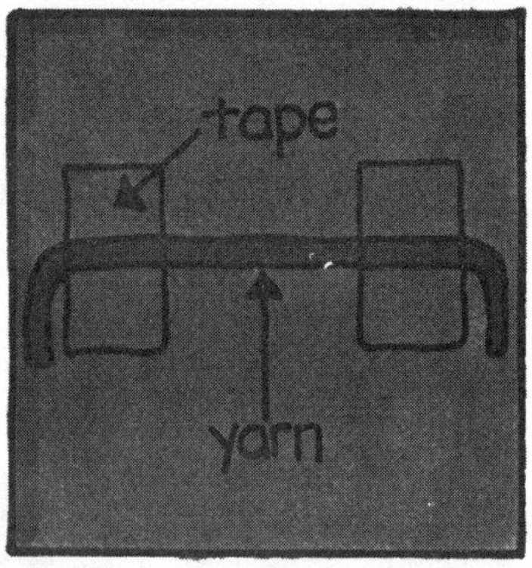


4. Pick a stamper. Use a paintbrush to lightly coat the shape with tempera paint. Don't put too much paint onto the shapes, or they will not print correctly. Slip two fingers under the yarn on the back and press it down onto a piece of white paper. Repeat this step with the other two stampers.

5. Use your imagination to fill up three pieces of white paper with prints. Make designs, patterns, etc. Put your name on each page and set them aside to dry.

6. Place the remaining clean sheet of paper horizontally and write your name in the center. Then put the other sheets underneath and paper-punch three holes on the left side (top, middle and bottom). Put the 6" (15.24 cm) yarn pieces through the holes and tie them into bows as shown to create your own print book. (Younger students will need assistance.)

# New Year's Dragon Puppet

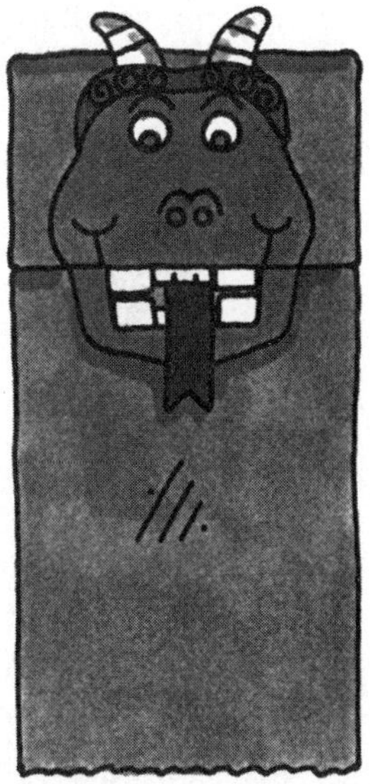

## Perfect Timing

Make this craft when studying China or reading:

- *Dragon Kites and Dragonflies: A Collection of Chinese Nursery Rhymes.* Demi. Harcourt Brace Jovanovich, 1986.
- *The Eyes of a Dragon.* Margaret Leaf. Lothrop, Lee & Shepard Books, 1987.
- *Everyone Knows What a Dragon Looks Like.* Jay Williams. Four Winds Press, 1976.

## Materials Needed

- used lunch bag*
- variety of colored paper circles
- reproducible dragon face patterns (page 23)
- crayons or washable markers
- red felt or construction paper strip
- glue
- scissors

## Tell the Class

"When the people in China celebrate the new year, they have a big festival. At this festival lots of people get together and carry a large, colorful dragon from underneath. Maybe you've seen this on television or in a book. Today you'll make a dragon puppet for yourself. When you're finished, you can take it home and use it to put on a show for your family."

## How to Make It

**For Teachers, Aides and Parent Volunteers**

**A.** Photocopy the dragon face patterns for each student.

**B.** Use a quarter and trace it many times onto a white sheet of photocopy paper. Then use this sheet to photocopy colored sheets of circles. (Colored photocopy paper is available at many print shops.) If your photocopier is sufficiently equipped, you can simply photocopy onto colored construction paper. Cut all the circles out. Place a generous amount into containers that three or four children can share.

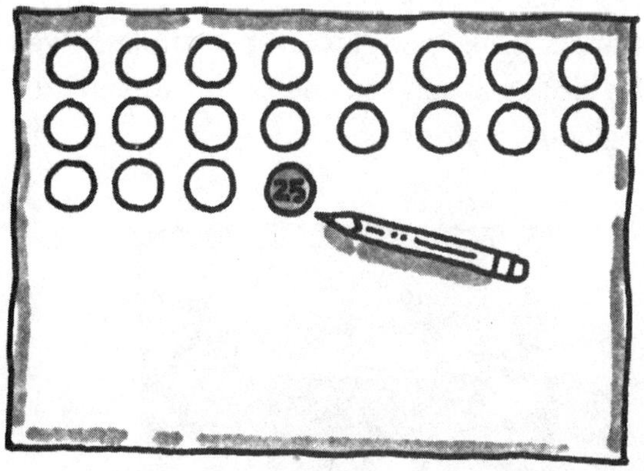


**C.** Cut ¾" x 2¾" (1.91 x 6.99 cm) pieces of red felt or construction paper. Every student will need one strip.

## How to Make It

**For Students**

**1.** Color and cut out the dragon face patterns.

2. Glue the dragon face to the lunch bag as shown.

3. Glue the colored paper circles to cover the entire back of the bag. Overlap each row as shown. (Only put glue on the upper halves of the circles. Then slip the circles under the unglued portions.)

4. Use scissors to notch a small piece out of the red felt or construction paper strip as shown.

Glue it under the flap of the bag as shown. Let the tongue dry, and then place the puppet on your hand and pretend you are leading it through a Chinese parade.

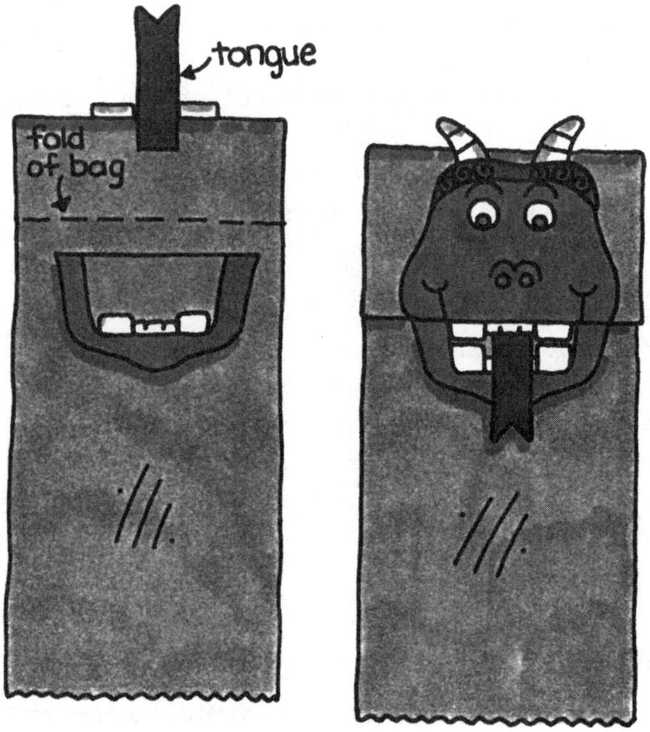

# Dragon Face Patterns

This pattern piece can be used as a tongue or a tail.

# Tricky Tangram Picture

## Perfect Timing

Make this craft when studying China or reading:

- *Chinese Mother Goose Rhymes.* Robert Wyndham. Philomel, 1982.
- *The Story About Ping.* Marjorie Flack and Kurt Wiese. Viking, 1933.
- *Mei Li.* Thomas Handforth. Doubleday, 1938.

## Materials Needed

- cereal box* (one box for each student)
- reproducible tangram pattern (page 26)
- crayons or washable markers
- scissors
- glue

## Tell the Class

Hold up a photocopy of the tangram puzzle pattern as you talk.

"A tangram is a Chinese puzzle that is made up of several different shapes. When the shapes are all put together in a certain way, they form a square. The tangram puzzle is hundreds of years old.

Today you will get to cut out the tangram puzzle pieces and use some of them to create pictures."

## How to Make It

**For Teachers, Aides and Parent Volunteers**

Photocopy a tangram pattern for each student.

## How to Make It

**For Students**

1. Cut off the front and back panels of the cereal box. (Younger students will need assistance.)

2. Glue the tangram pattern onto the blank side of one of the cereal box panels. Let it dry and then cut the pieces out.

3. Use your imagination to arrange some of the pieces into a picture. (Younger students can use only one piece and incorporate it into a drawing if they want.) Glue the picture onto the blank side of the remaining cereal box panel. If tangram pieces don't want to lay flat, put some heavy books on top of your picture for a while.

(butterfly)

4. Draw any details (such as the trunk of a pine tree), and draw in a background if you want.

**Note:** There are many tangram patterns and activity books available. Check your local school supply store or library.

# Tangram

# Straw on the String Game

## Perfect Timing

Make this craft when studying Colombia.

## Materials Needed

These directions are for just one "straw on the string" that will be used by all students.

- drinking straw (used but rinsed out)*
- about 20' (6.1 m) string (You can knot scraps of string together to achieve this length if you like.)
- scissors

## Tell the Class

"In Colombia there is a popular game that uses a long piece of string with a ring on it. The children pass, or pretend to pass, the ring to each other. One child is 'it' and tries to guess who has the ring when the passing stops.

Today we're going to make and then play a game that is something like this."

## How to Make It

### For Teachers, Aides and Parent Volunteers

**A.** Cut a 1" (2.54 cm) piece from the straw. Put the string through the straw and knot the ends together.

**B.** Read the instructions given to the students so you will know what you need to do.

## How to Play It

Play the game as follows:

1. The teacher chooses a child to be "it." This child closes her eyes. The other children should form a circle around the child that is "it" while holding the string in front of them. The teacher will explain that when the game starts, the student with the straw should pass it to the student on either side of them, at which time that student should pass it to another and so on. Those children without the straw should pretend to pass it anyway to try to fool the child who is "it."

2. The game begins when the teacher shouts, "Slide that straw!" After the children begin passing the straw from one to another, the teacher should tell the child who is "it" that they can open their eyes and watch the others.

3. The passing of the straw continues for three minutes until the teacher says "Stop!"

4. The child who is "it" then says, "Who has the straw? I wish I knew! Angela, Angela, (or whatever the name of the child she guesses is) is it you?" If the child has guessed correctly, then she joins the circle and the child who had the straw becomes "it." If the child guessed incorrectly, she remains "it" for another game. If the child who is "it" guesses incorrectly a second time, she should join the circle and the teachers should name another child to be "it."

# Cascading Cascarones

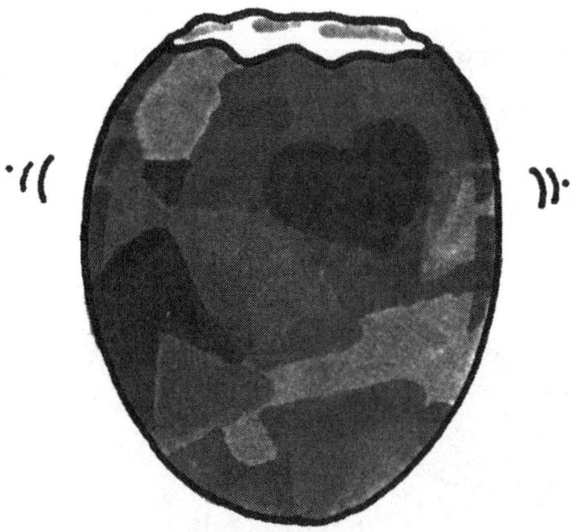

## Perfect Timing

Make this craft when studying Guatemala or reading:

- *The Most Beautiful Place in the World.* Ann Cameron. Knopf, 1988.
- *Abuela's Weave.* Omar S. Castaneda. Lee & Low Books, 1993.

### Materials Needed

- hollow eggshell (Have students transport an egg to school in an egg carton.)
- piece of newspaper*
- zip-to-seal bag
- strips and shapes of art tissue (Art tissue can be found in art supply stores and comes packaged in a variety of vivid colors.)
- paper punch
- glue
- scissors
- shallow bowls

## Tell the Class

"In Guatemala people fill hollow decorated eggs with confetti. They are called *cascarones*. They hold it over a friend's head, break it and shake all the confetti out. This is done as a symbol of affection.

You will have the chance to make your own confetti-filled egg. While you work, think of a friend that you would like to shake the confetti on."

## How to Make It

**For Teachers, Aides and Parent Volunteers**

This craft takes two days to complete. Do step A the first day.

**A.** Have each student bring you his egg and then carefully poke a hole into the end with the point of a pair of scissors. (Be sure you don't crack the entire egg.) Move the tip of the scissors in a circular motion to make the opening large enough so that the student can easily fill it with confetti. Discard the inside of the egg, rinse it out and leave it to dry overnight.

**B.** Tear art tissue into small strips about $1\frac{1}{4}$" x $\frac{1}{2}$" (3.18 x 1.27 cm). Cut some small shapes (like hearts, triangles and stars) from it also. Place a generous amount of strips and shapes into bowls that students can share (six per bowl).

**C.** Mix glue and water together until it is runny. Put the mixture into shallow bowls that students can share (three per bowl).

**D.** Cut newspaper pages into fourths. Each student will need one fourth.

## How to Make It

**For Students**

This craft takes two days to complete. Do steps 1 and 2 on the first day.

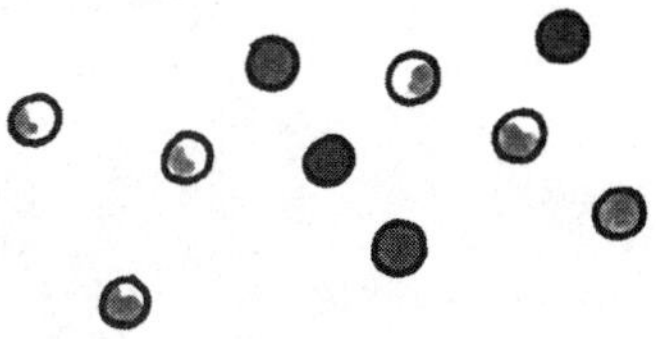

1. Use a paper punch to make confetti from the piece of newspaper. Store the confetti in a zip-to-seal bag.

2. Dip the art tissue strips and shapes, one at a time, into the glue mixture. Place them on the egg. It's alright to overlap the strips and shapes. This will cause the colors to mix together. Immediately after covering the entire eggshell, pull the strips and shapes off. The pigment of the tissue will remain. Let your eggshell dry overnight.

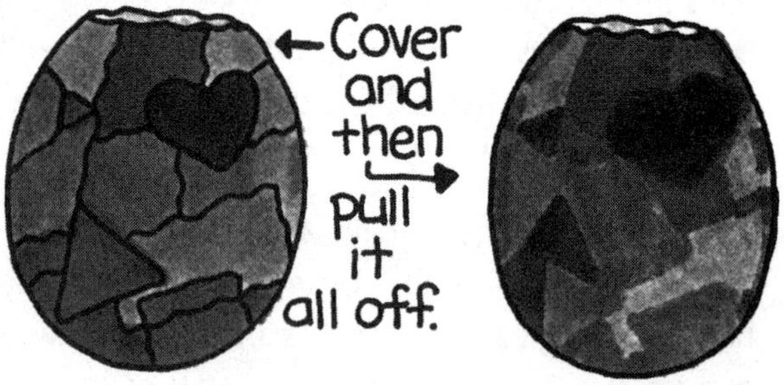


3. The next day, carefully fill your egg with confetti.

4. Go to a large area (where it will be easy to sweep up later) with your egg and a friend. Have your friend kneel down. Shake the confetti over your friend's head.

5. While you shake your egg, you may want to talk about why you like your friend. (For example, "You're funny and lots of fun on the playground.")

# Dipas Raft

## Perfect Timing

Make this craft when studying India or reading:

- *The Monkey and the Crocodile: A Jataka Tale from India.* Paul Galdone. Clarion Books, 1969.
- *A Journey to Paradise.* Anne Siberell. H. Holt, 1990.
- *Once a Mouse.* Marcia Brown. Scribner, 1961.

## Materials Needed

- Styrofoam™ tray*
- drinking straw* (Two students can share one.)
- modeling clay (small lump)
- yellow construction paper scraps
- waterproof markers or acrylic paints
- tape
- scissors

## Tell the Class

"In India, Hindus celebrate a festival of lights called Diwali. The children make Dipas which are small, clay oil lamps. Sometimes the children place these lamps on rafts and sail them across a river. They believe if the raft reaches the other side while the lamp is still burning, their families will have good luck in the coming year.

Today we're going to make our own Dipas rafts. Later, as you watch yours float, tell me what good things you are hoping for."

## How to Make It

**For Teachers, Aides and Parent Volunteers**

**A.** Cut all the drinking straws in half. Give one half to each student.

**B.** Fill a large dishpan half full of water in which children can float their rafts.

## How to Make It

**For Students**

1. Cut a teardrop shape from a yellow construction paper scrap. Tape it to the top of the straw. This is the candle. (Younger students will need assistance.)

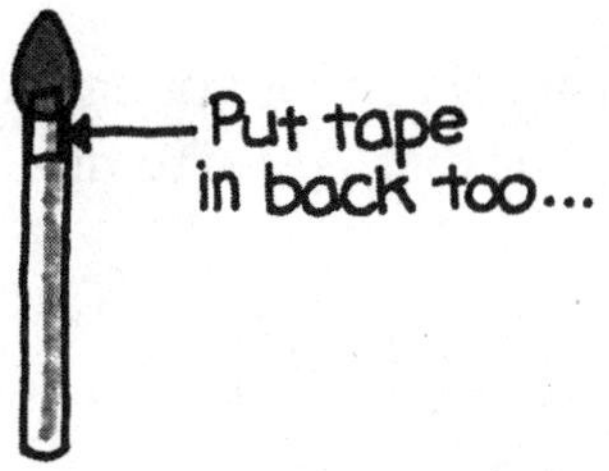


2. Roll the lump of clay into a small ball and press it down firmly onto the middle of the Styrofoam™ tray. Stick the candle into it so that it is standing upright.

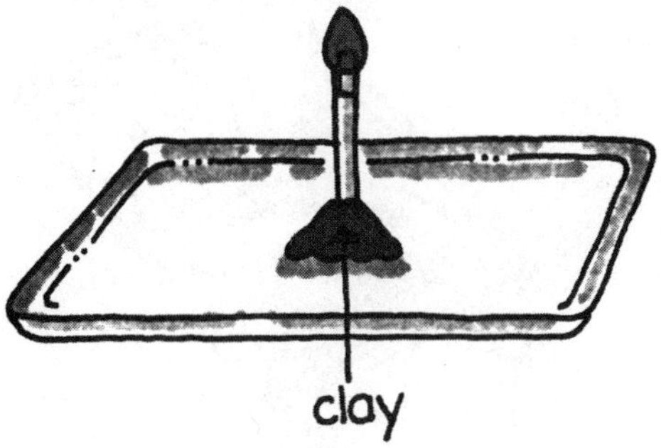

3. Write your name on a scrap of yellow paper and tape it onto the raft.

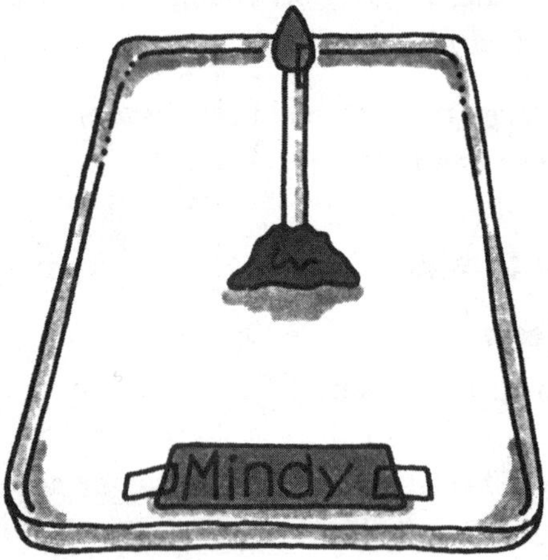


4. Use waterproof markers or acrylic paint to decorate your raft. Allow to dry.

5. Place your raft in the dishpan to float. Tell your teacher about something you are hoping for. For example, "I hope I get a puppy" or "I hope my little brother gets over his cold."

6. Take your raft home and as a family watch it float in the kitchen sink. Tell each member of your family what you hoped for them at school. For example, "Jason, I hoped you would get lots of home runs when you play baseball next season."

# Behold Our Beautiful Buttons

## Perfect Timing

Make this craft when studying Italy or reading:

- *Tony's Bread: An Italian Folktale*. Tomie de Paola. Putnam, 1989.
- *The Mysterious Giant of Barletta*. Tomie de Paola. Harcourt Brace Jovanovich, 1984.
- *The Talking Tree*. Inna Rayesky. Putnam, 1989.

## Materials Needed

- 3 large, flat buttons
- yarn
- large brown grocery bag* (Two students can share one.)
- magazines (with lots of pictures of flowers)*
- seed catalogs (with lots of pictures of flowers)*
- reproducible shirt pattern (page 35)
- crayons or washable markers
- glue
- scissors

## Tell the Class

"Italian artists make beautiful buttons using a method called *millefiori* which means "a thousand flowers." For many years this method was kept a secret. We'll learn a way to make our own beautiful buttons and then glue them onto a pretend shirt."

## How to Make It

**For Teachers, Aides and Parent Volunteers**

**A.** Make a photocopy of the shirt pattern for each student.

**B.** Cut 8" (20.32 cm) pieces of yarn. Each student will need one.

**C.** Prepare a space on the wall or a bulletin board entitled "Behold Our Beautiful Buttons!" You can display the finished crafts in this area.

## How to Make It

**For Students**

**1.** Cut the front and back panels off a large brown grocery bag. Keep one of the panels and give the other to a classmate to use.

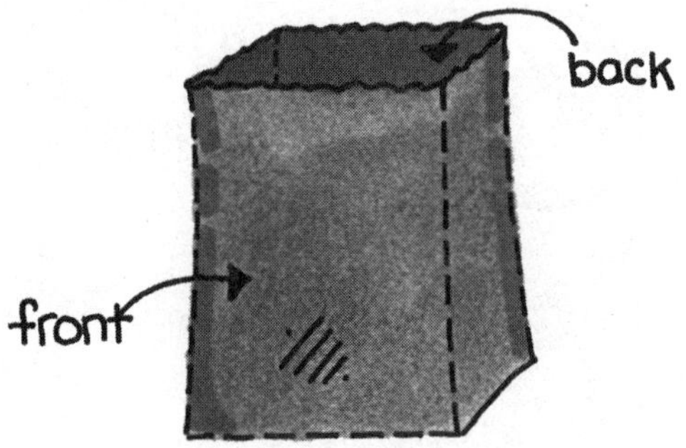


**2.** Cut out the shirt pattern. Trace it onto the grocery bag panel and cut it out. If there is a logo printed on your panel, flip it over and use the blank side.

3. Draw a collar and a line down the middle. Use crayons or markers to decorate the shirt with stripes, hearts, dots, a plaid pattern, etc.

4. Cut three small colorful flowers from a magazine or seed catalog. Glue them onto the buttons.

5. Glue the decorated buttons onto the shirt.

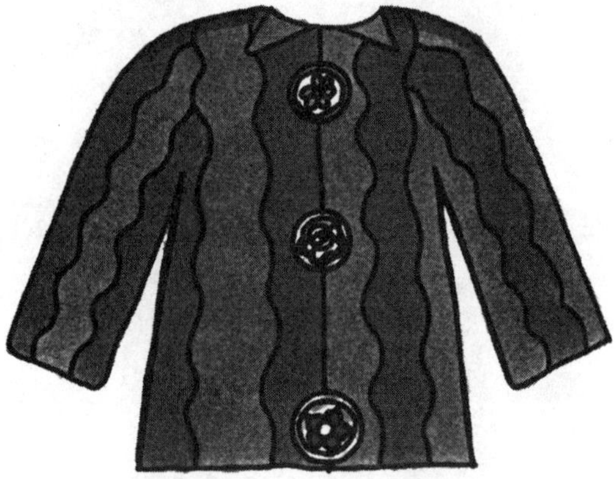

6. Tape the piece of yarn onto the back of the shirt to serve as a hanger. (Younger students will need assistance.)

7. Let your teacher display your shirt and its beautiful buttons!

**Option:** To make a pin (for a gift), first sew a safety pin to the back of a button or glue it on. Decorate the front as described. When dry, coat with clear nail polish or shellac.

# Shirt Pattern

# "Fan"tastic Japanese Fan

## ■ Perfect Timing

Make this craft when studying Japan or reading:

- *The Badger and the Magic Fan.* Tony Johnston. Putnam, 1990.
- *The Magic Fan.* Keith Baker. Harcourt Brace Jovanovich, 1989.
- *The Tongue-Cut Sparrow.* Momoko Ishii. Lodestar Books, 1987.

## ■ Materials Needed

- craft sticks*
- reproducible fan pattern (page 38)
- reproducible stick placement guide (page 39)
- crayons or washable markers
- glue
- scissors

## ■ Tell the Class

If possible, bring a Japanese fan to the classroom.

"The Japanese folding fan, called sensu, was invented long ago by a Japanese craftsman. This craftsman designed the fan to fold like the wings of a bat. These fans became very popular with the Japanese people. Often emperors would give them as gifts. These fans come in lots of colors and with many different designs on them.

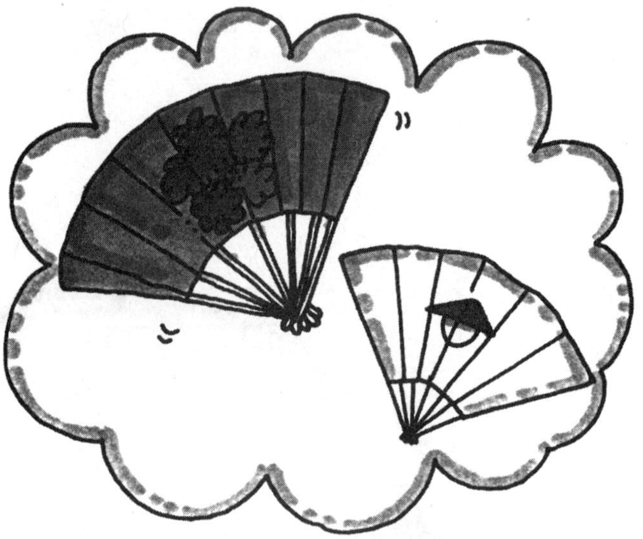

The fan you are going to make will have a picture of a bonsai tree on it. This type of tree is grown in Japan and is made to stay very small."

## ■ How to Make It

**For Teachers, Aides and Parent Volunteers**

**A.** Photocopy the fan pattern and the stick placement guide. Every student will need one of each.

**B.** (This craft will take two days to complete. Do this step on the first day.) Demonstrate how to lay the craft sticks on top of the stick placement guide as directed. Have students glue the sticks together (being careful not to glue them to the guide) and let them dry overnight. (Younger students will need you to do this for them.)

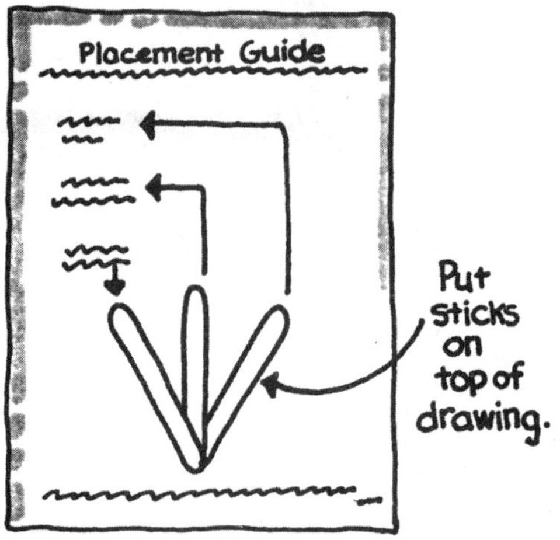

## ■ How to Make It

**For Students**

On the second day:

1. Color and cut out the fan pattern.
2. Fold the entire fan accordion style (back and forth) on the lines provided. (Younger students will need assistance.)

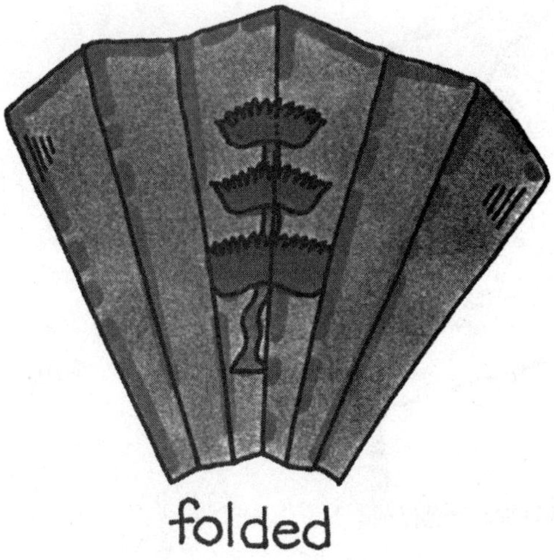


3. Remove the craft sticks from the stick placement guide and glue them to the bottom of the fan as shown. Leave 2" (5.08 cm) of the sticks extended from the bottom to serve as a handle. Secure each side with a piece of tape. (Students may need assistance.)

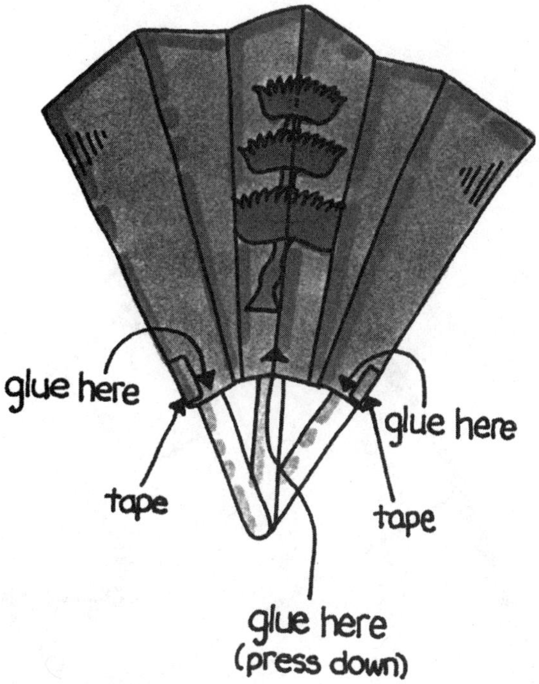


4. Take your fan home and display it proudly!

# Japanese Fan Pattern

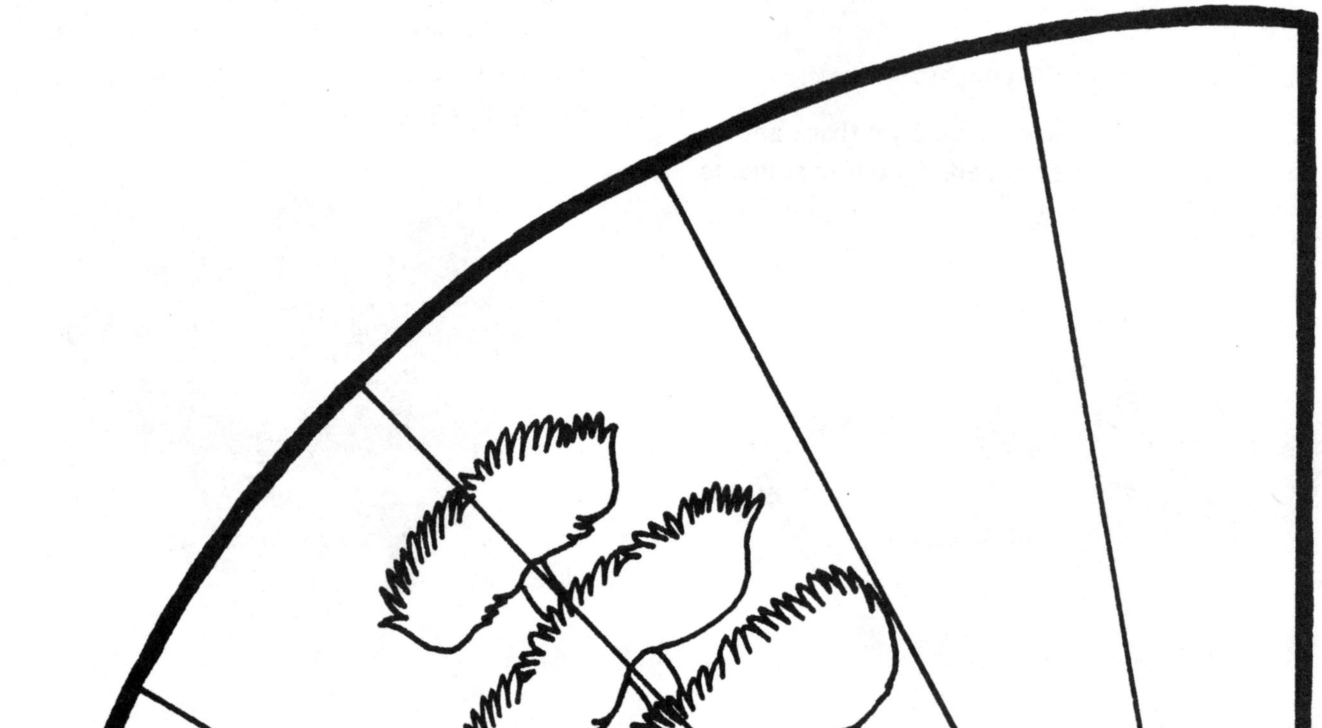

# Stick Placement Guide

Place the first stick here.

Glue the second stick on top of the first . . .

and the third stick on top of the second.

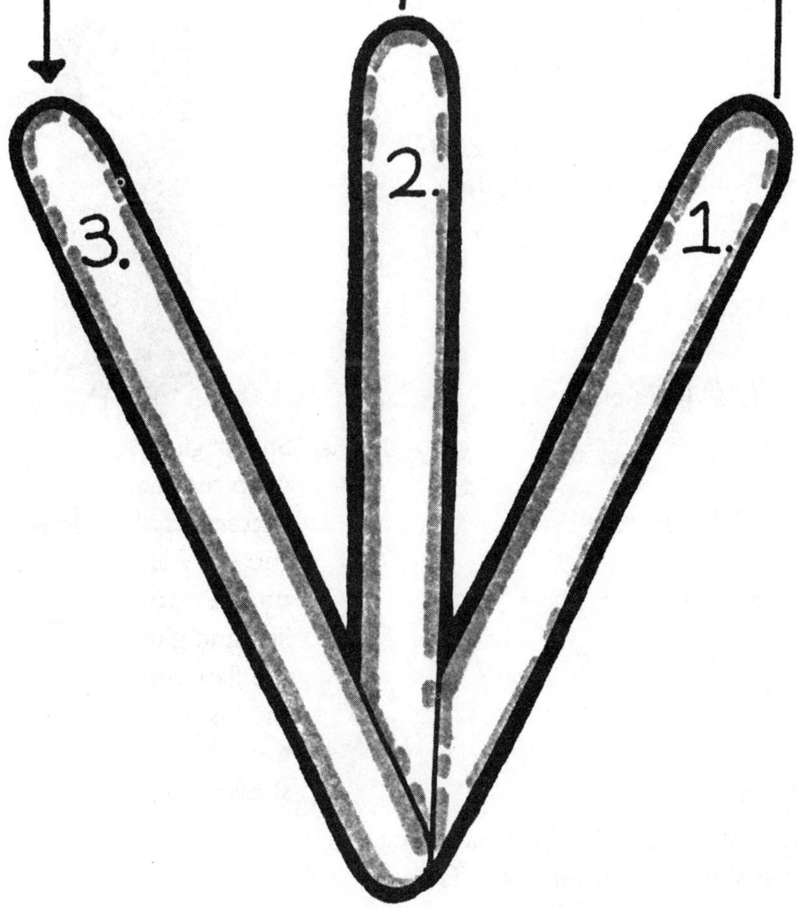

# Rice Field-Worker

## Perfect Timing

Make this craft when studying Japan or reading:

- *Momtaro: Peach Boy.* George Suyeoka. Island Heritage, 1972.
- *The Stonecutter.* Gerald McDermott. Viking, 1975.
- *The Boy of the Three-Year Nap.* Dianne Snyder. Houghton Mifflin, 1988.

## Materials Needed

- toilet tissue tube*
- paper cupcake liner (2½" [6.35 cm])
- reproducible rice field-worker and feet pattern (page 42)
- crayons or washable markers
- tape
- rice (¼ teaspoon [1.25 ml])
- scraps of black yarn
- glue
- scissors

## Tell the Class

"In Japan people eat a lot of rice. Workers have to pick the rice from fields where it is very hot. The workers help protect themselves from the sun by wearing large straw hats. I'll show you how to make a pretend rice field-worker that wears a special hat."

## How to Make It

**For Teachers, Aides and Parent Volunteers**

Photocopy a pattern of the rice field-worker for each student.

## How to Make It

**For Students**

1. Color the rice field-worker and feet pattern and cut them out.
2. Glue the rice field-worker around the toilet tissue tube. Tape the seam together.

3. Smear glue onto the feet pattern as shown. Fold on the dotted line and glue the flap onto the inside of the tube as shown.

4. Glue black yarn scraps onto the hair area.

5. Place the cupcake liner onto the top of the tube and tape it in place.

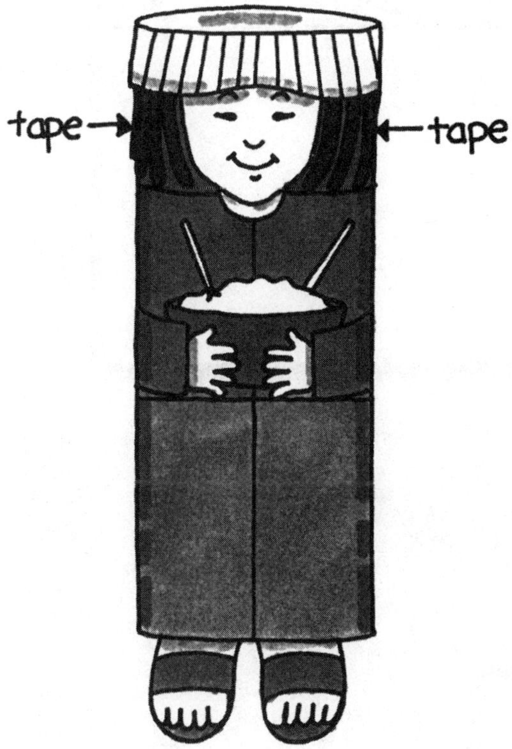


6. Glue some rice onto the bowl that the rice field-worker is holding.

7. Take your creation home and tell your family how you made it!

# Rice Field-Worker Pattern

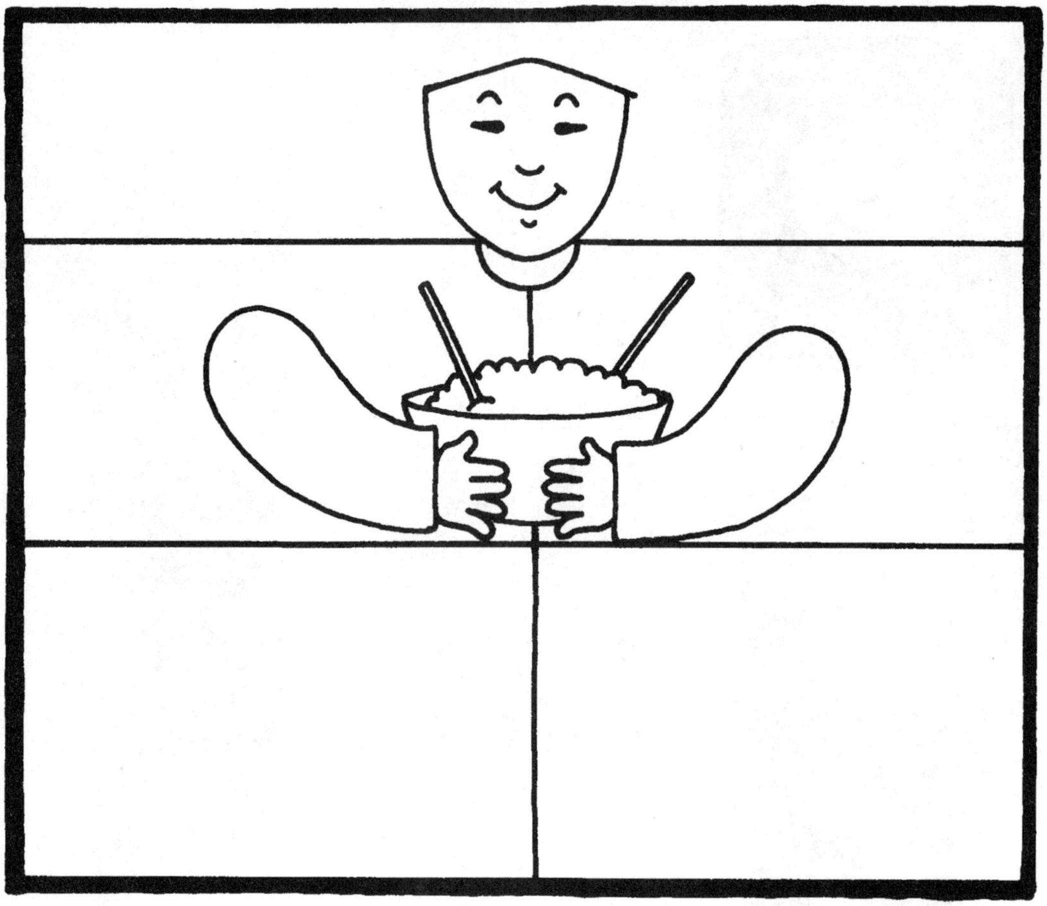

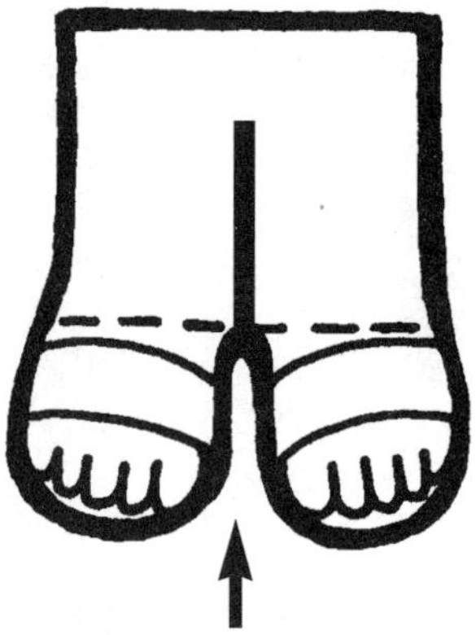

**Cut on solid line between feet.**

# Cinch Chomsŏngdale Observatory

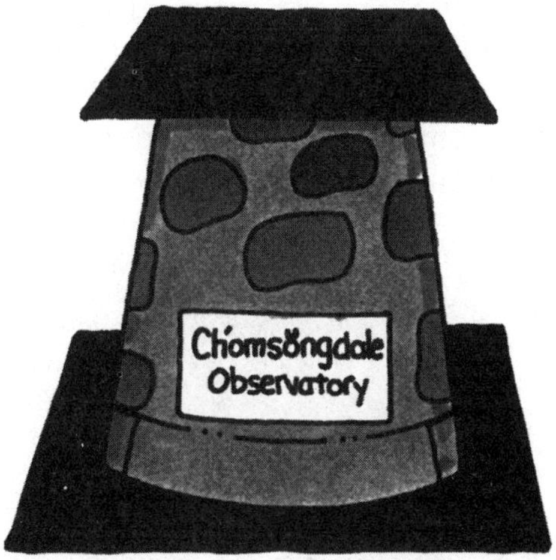


## Perfect Timing

Make this craft when studying Korea or reading:

- *Tales of a Korean Grandmother.* Frances Carpenter. Tuttle, 1972.
- *The Korean Cinderella.* Shirley Climo. HarperCollins Publishers, 1993.
- *The Chinese Mirror: Adapted from a Korean Folktale.* Mirra Ginsburg. Harcourt Brace Jovanovich, 1988.

## Materials Needed

- Styrofoam™ cup*
- reproducible Chomsŏngdale Observatory pattern (page 45)
- gray, tan, brown and brick red crayons
- 2 black construction paper squares
- fine-grain sand
- scissors
- glue

## Tell the Class

"An observatory is a building in which people can study the stars and sky. The stars and sky are very important to the Korean people. The Chomsŏngdale (pronounced chom-sung-deh) Observatory is a famous building in Korea. It might be the oldest observatory in the world. It is made with 365 stones. Each one represents a day of the year. It stands 29 feet (8.84 m) tall.

I'll show you a way to make a model of this observatory."

## How to Make It

**For Teachers, Aides and Parent Volunteers**

**A.** Cut 4" x 4" (10.16 x 10.16 cm) and 3" x 3" (7.62 x 7.62 cm) squares from black construction paper. Each student will need one of each size.

**B.** Photocopy an observatory pattern for each student.

## How to Make It

**For Students**

1. Use a tan crayon to color the Styrofoam™ cup.
2. Use gray, brown and brick red crayons to color all the stones on the observatory pattern page. You don't need to color the Chomsŏngdale Observatory sign.
3. Glue the sign to the cup as shown.

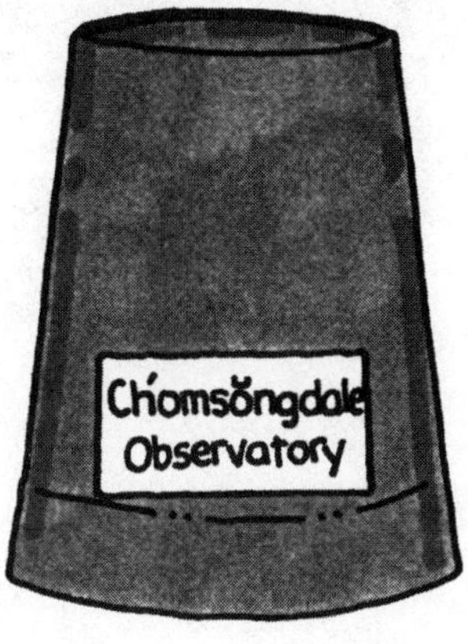

4. Glue the stones onto the cup. Glue them quite close to one another. Don't glue any to the bottom.

5. Smear glue around the rim of the cup. Place it firmly onto the center of the larger black construction paper square. Secure it by taping the sides down.

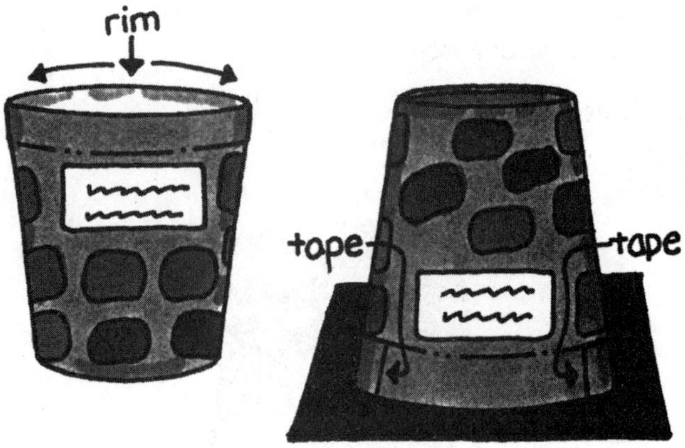


6. Spread a generous amount of glue onto the bottom of the cup (including the little rim). Place the small black construction paper square on the bottom of the cup as shown.

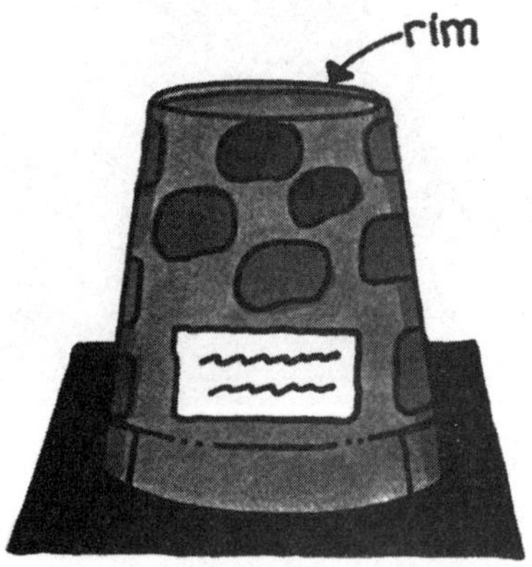

7. Take it home and tell your family about the real observatory in Korea.

# Ch́omsŏngdale Observatory Pattern

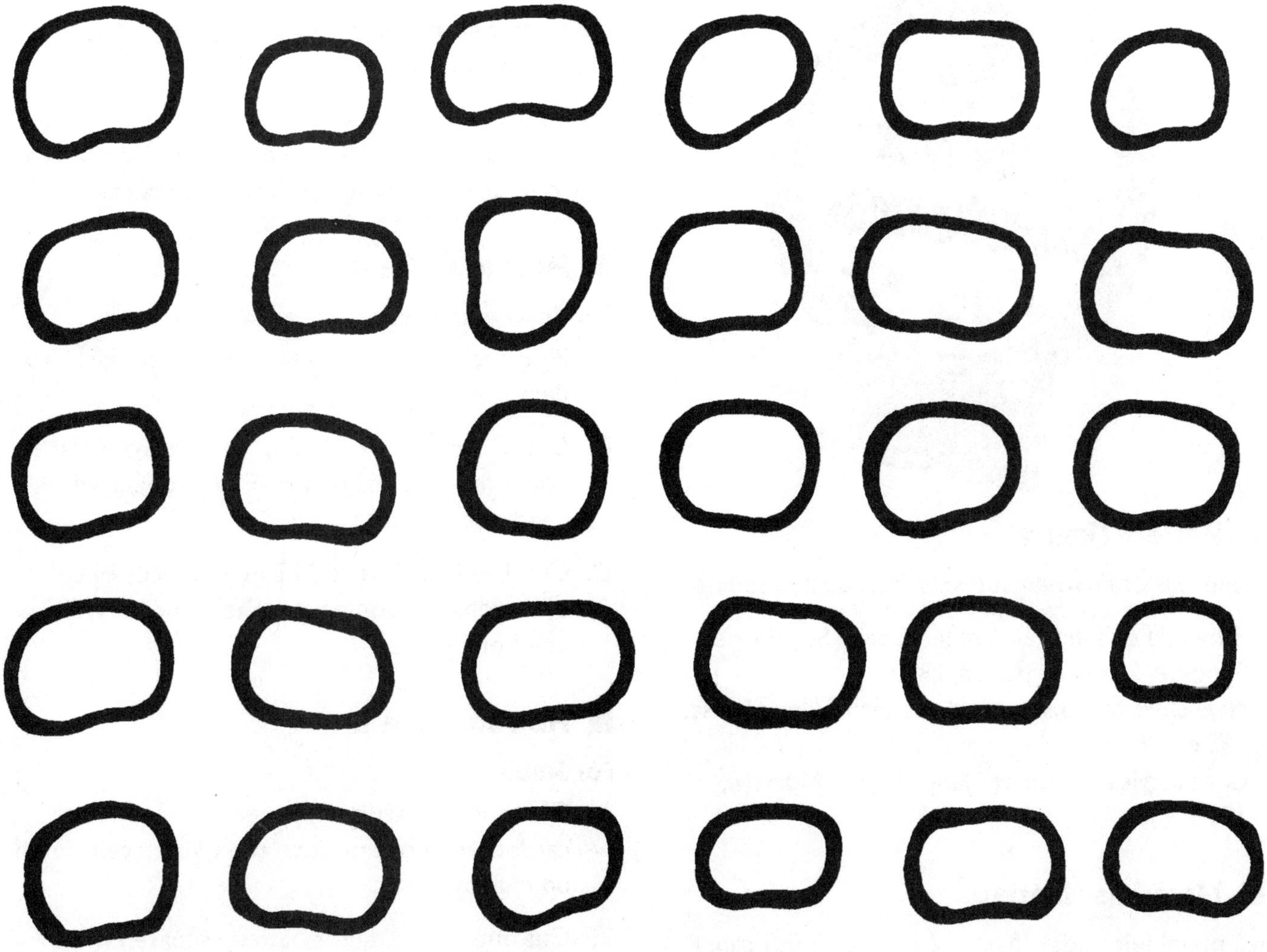

**Ch́omsŏngdale Observatory**

# Colorful Castanets

## ■ Perfect Timing

Make this craft when studying Mexico or reading:

- *Esmerald and the Pet Parade.* Cecile Schoberle. Simon & Schuster Books, 1990.
- *Nine Days to Christmas.* Marie Hall. Viking Press, 1959.
- *Gus the Mexican Ghost.* Jane Thayer. Morrow, 1974.

## ■ Materials Needed

- 2 metal juice lids* (from 12 oz. [354.9 ml] cans)
- cereal box* (One can be shared by two students.)
- reproducible castanets patterns (page 48)
- piece of construction paper
- crayons or washable markers
- masking tape
- glue
- scissors

## ■ Tell the Class

If possible, bring an authentic set of castanets to class so students can see and hear them.

"Mexico is home to many talented musicians. Some of these musicians use an instrument called castanets. It makes noise when its two round parts are tapped against each other. Castanets from Mexico are often carved from wood.

I will show you a way to make castanets using juice lids and cardboard. When we are finished, we can play our castanets along with some Mexican music."

## ■ How to Make It

**For Teachers, Aides and Parent Volunteers**

**A.** Photocopy the castanets patterns for each student.

**B.** Cut 4" x 8" (10.16 x 20.32 cm) pieces of cardboard from cereal boxes. Each student will need one.

**C.** Cut 4" x 8" (10.16 x 20.32 cm) pieces of colored construction paper. Each student will need one piece.

## ■ How to Make It

**For Students**

1. Glue the construction paper to the piece of cardboard. Position it so the two pieces match up exactly. Let it dry.
2. Cut out the castanets pattern square on the dotted lines. Glue it as shown to the blank side

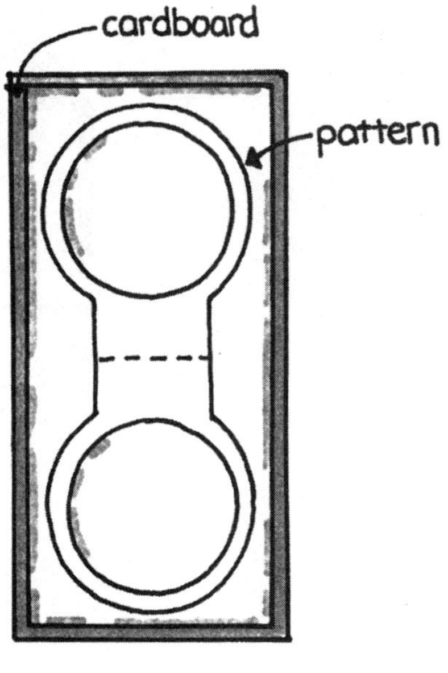

of the cardboard. Set it aside to dry.

3. Color the two circles and cut them out. Cut

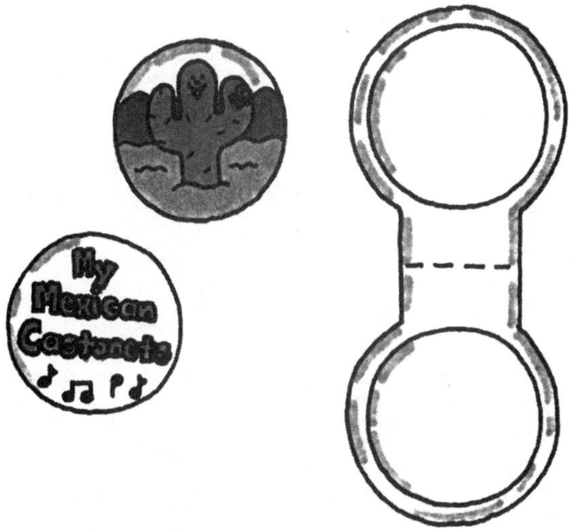


out the castanets pattern (which is now glued on the cardboard).

4. Flip the castanets pattern over so that the col-

ored side (with the construction paper) is showing. Glue the circles on as shown.

5. Flip your castanets pattern over so that the pat-

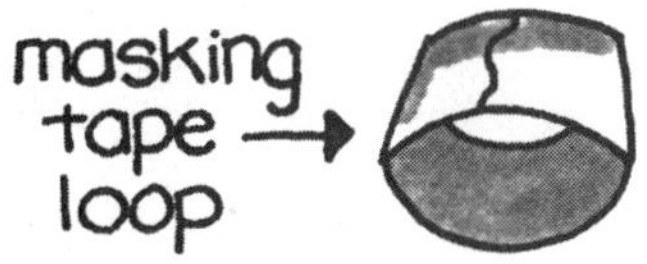


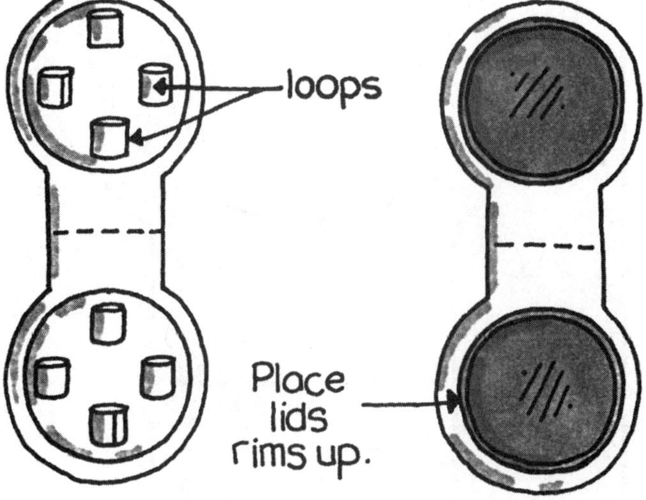


tern side is showing. Put four loops of masking tape on each blank circle area. Press juice lids onto the tape.

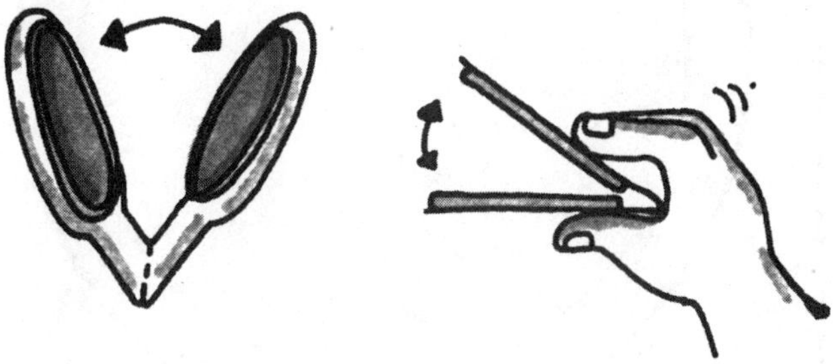

6. Fold the castanets on the dotted line so that the two lids meet. Hold as shown and open and close to make clicking noise.

# Castanets Patterns

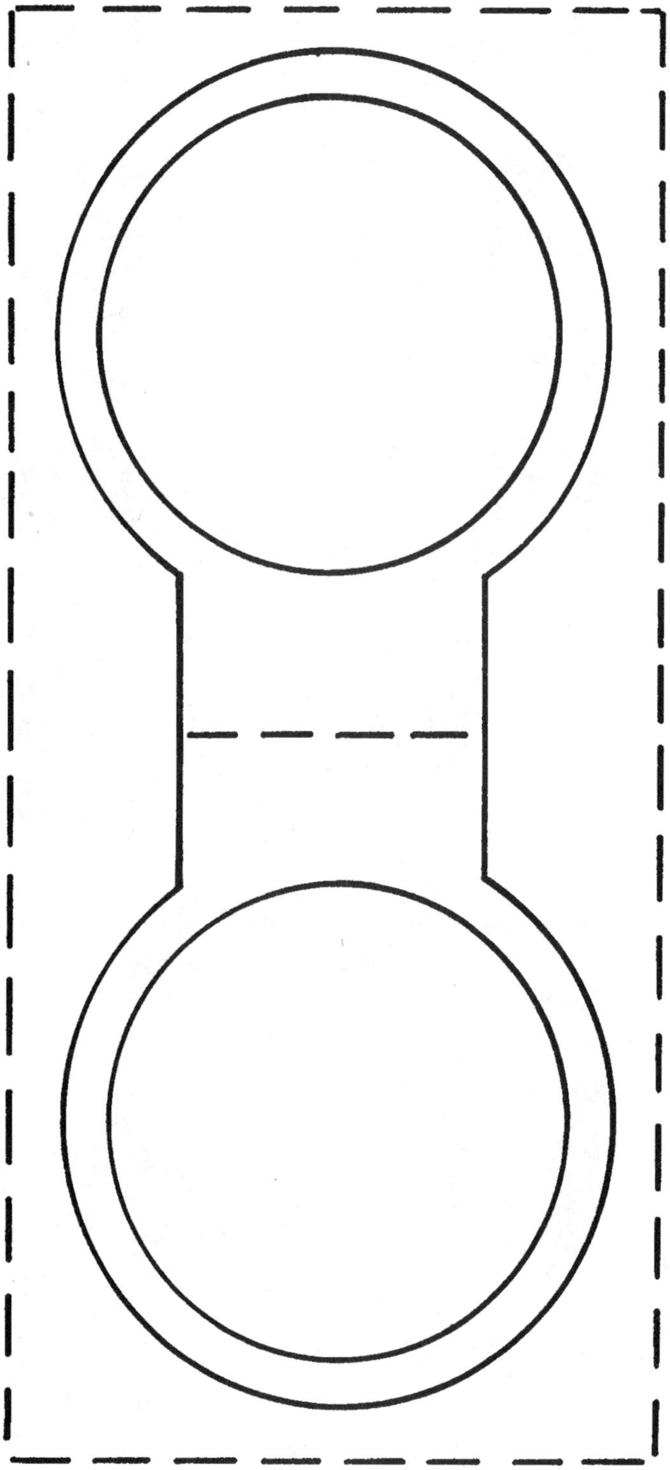

# Gorgeous God's Eye

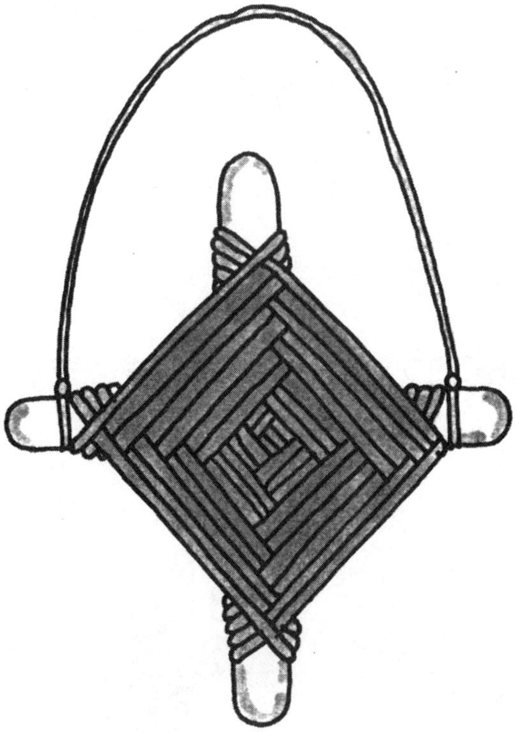

## Perfect Timing

Make this craft when studying Mexico or reading:

- *Mystery of the Maya.* R.A. Montgomery. Grey Castle Press, 1987.
- *The Nicest Gift.* Leo Politi. Scribner, 1973.
- *Santiago's Silver Mine.* Eleanor Lawenton Clymer. Atheneum, 1973.

## Materials Needed

- 2 craft sticks*
- cardboard of yarn
- piece of yarn
- glue
- scissors

## Tell the Class

If possible, bring a few completed God's eyes to class.

"A God's eye is a decorative craft made from sticks and yarn. In Mexico they call a God's eye an *Ojo de Dios.* Some Mexican people believe they will bring them good luck.

We're going to make our own God's eyes in this class. It's fairly easy. Once you learn how to make one, you can show other members of your family at home."

## How to Make It

**For Teachers, Aides and Parent Volunteers**

This craft takes two days to complete. Do step A the first day.

**A.** Show your students how to glue one stick on top of the other to make a plus symbol. As your students do this, walk around and supervise this process. (Younger students may need you to do this for them.) Let them dry overnight.

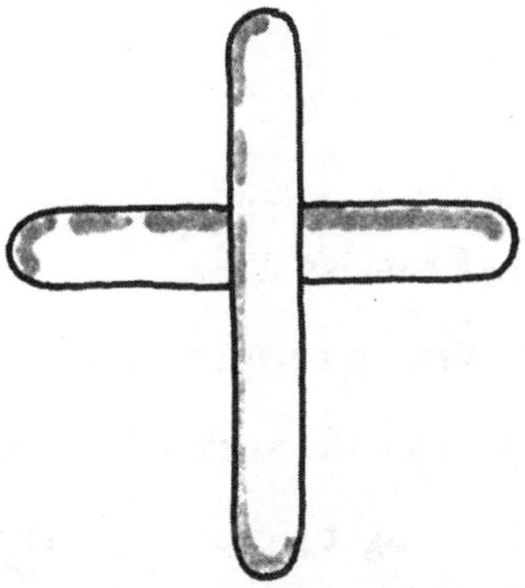

**B.** Unwind yarn onto rectangles of cardboard. Every student will need one cardboard with enough yarn to make a God's eye.

C. Cut 12" (30.48 cm) pieces of yarn. Every student will need one piece.

D. Practice the instructions given to students until you are easily able to make a God's eye.

## ■ How to Make It

### For Students

1. Knot the end of the yarn around the center of the cross as shown. (Students will need assistance.)

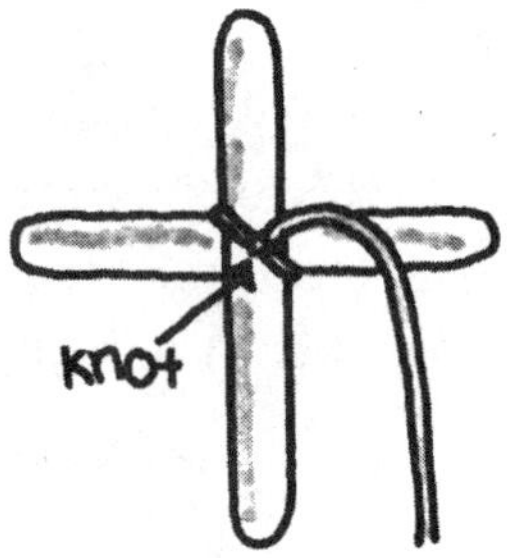


2. If you need help with any of the following steps, your teacher can assist you.

   **a.** Pull the yarn up to your right.

   **b.** Wrap it under the stick and to your left.

   **c.** Pull it down tightly, crossing over the center to the right.

   **d.** Turn the cross one quarter counter-clockwise and pull the yarn up.

   **e.** Once again, wrap it under the stick and to your left.

   **f.** Once again, pull it down tightly, crossing over the center to the right.
   Continue repeating steps d through f. As you wrap, take care to keep the yarn moving up the sticks.

   **g.** Keep wrapping. Eventually a diamond pattern will appear.

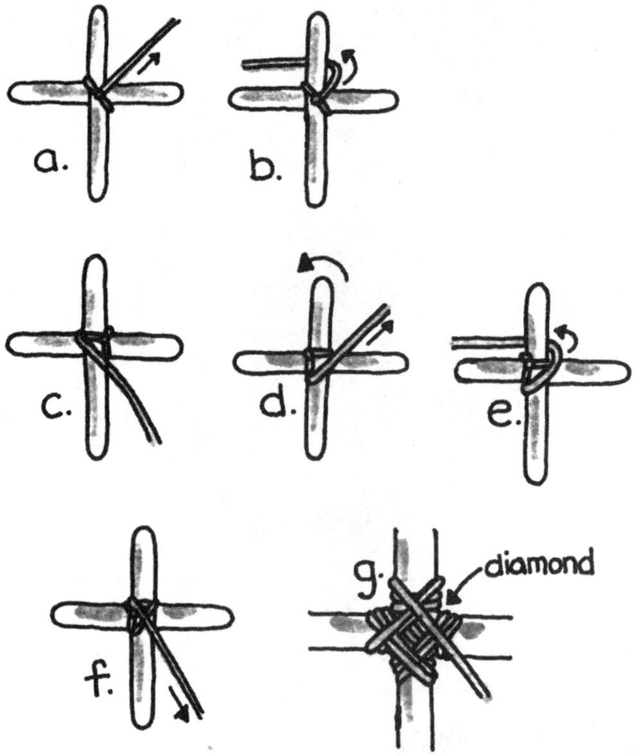


3. When only ½" (1.27 cm) of the sticks are showing, tie and knot the yarn onto the nearest stick. Then tie and knot both ends of the single piece of yarn onto the God's eye as shown to make a hanger. (Students will need assistance.)

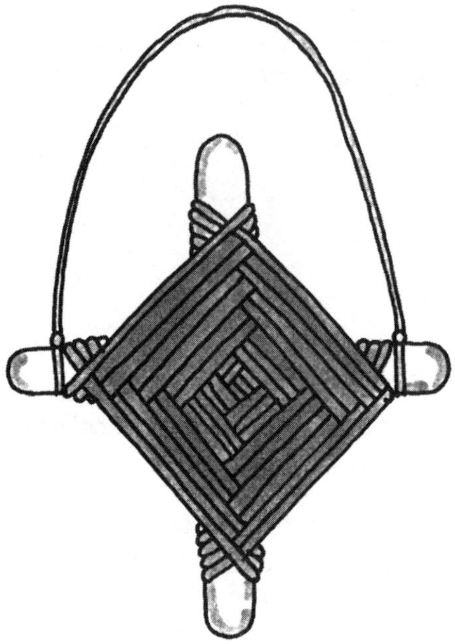

# Lovely Lid Mosaic

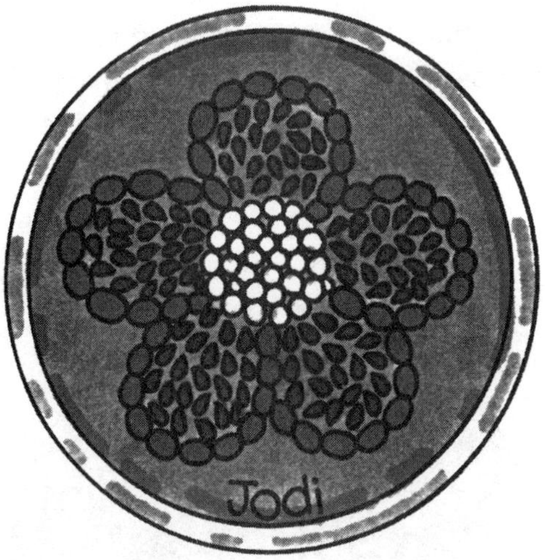


## Perfect Timing

Make this craft when studying Mexico or reading:

- *Borreguita and the Coyote: A Tale from Ayutla, Mexico.* Verna Aardema. Knopf, 1991.
- *Pedro and the Padre: A Tale from Jalisco, Mexico.* Verna Aardema. Dial Books for Young Readers, 1991.
- *The Tale of Rabbit and Coyote.* Tony Johnston. Putnam, 1994.

## Materials Needed

- molding dough (very soft and easy for young children to work with)
- sharp pencil
- shallow bowls
- nondairy topping lid* (8" [20.32 cm] diameter)
- beads, split peas, mixed beans and small seeds

## Tell the Class

If possible, bring some type of mosaic to the classroom.

"A mosaic is a picture or a design that has been made by placing little items (like tiles, beads or stones) into a soft surface. The Huichol Indians, who live in North-Central Mexico, are famous for their beautiful mosaics.

Put on your thinking caps and imagine a small picture or design that you can make as your mosaic."

## How to Make It

**For Teachers, Aides and Parent Volunteers**

Put an assortment of beads, split peas, mixed beans and small seeds into shallow bowls that students can share (three per bowl).

## How to Make It

**For Students**

1. Spread the dough evenly all over the plastic lid until it is covered.

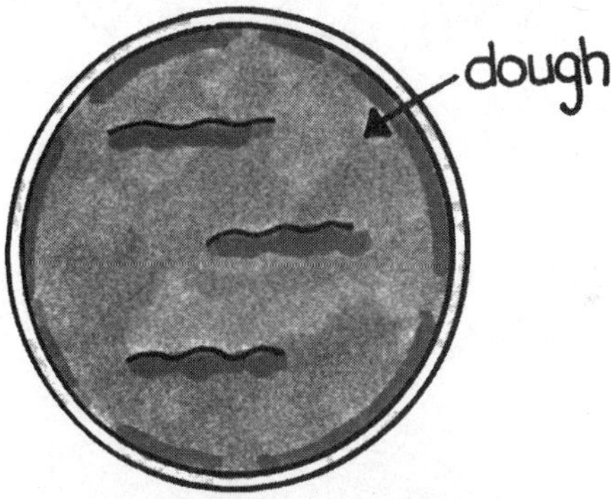


2. Use the sharp pencil to draw a simple picture (like a house or sailboat), a design or a shape (such as a star or diamond) into the dough.

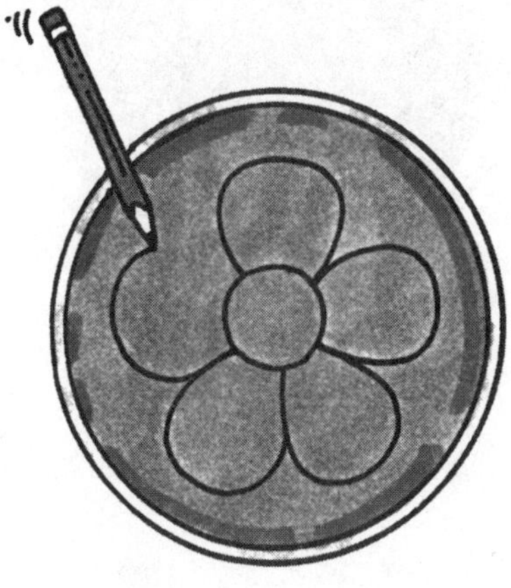

3. Choose from the items provided (beads, peas, etc.) to press into the outline of your picture.

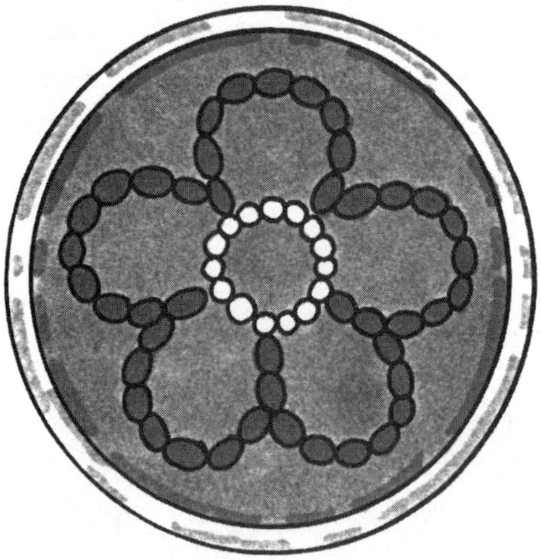

4. Use the items provided (beads, peas, etc.) to fill in the rest of your picture.

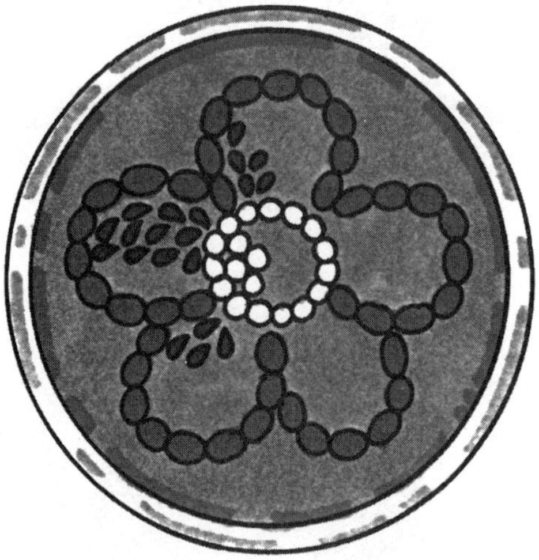

5. Use the pencil again to write your name into your mosaic. Let it dry until it is hard. Take it home and put it someplace where everyone can admire it.

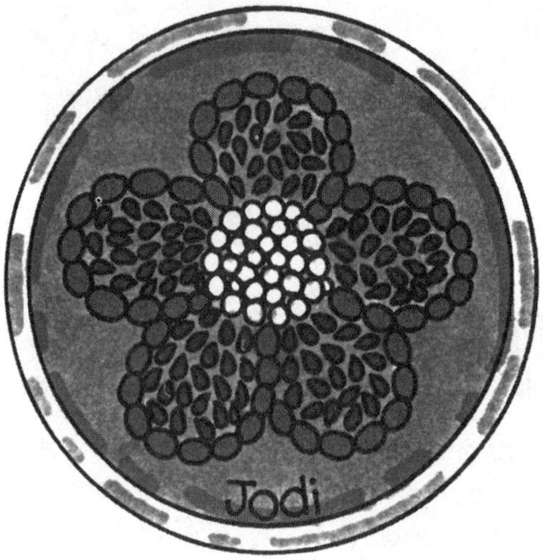

# Magnificent Mexican Poncho

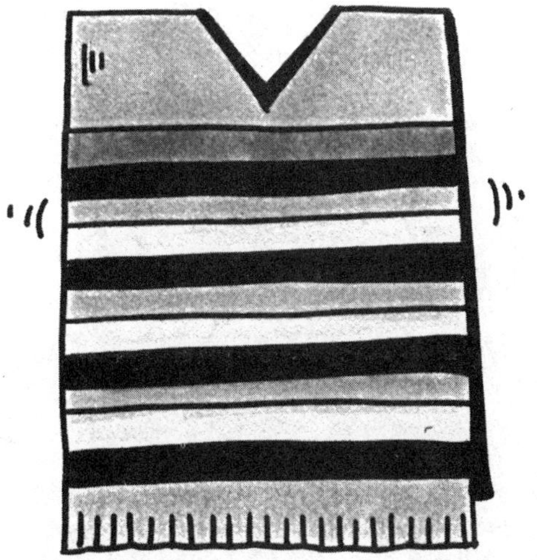

## Perfect Timing

Make this craft when studying Mexico or reading:

- *The Legend of the Poinsettia.* Tomie de Paola. Putnam, 1994.
- *The Mouse Bride: A Mayan Folktale.* Judith Dupre. Knopf, 1993.
- *A Quetzalcoatl Tale of Corn.* Marilyn Parke and Sharon Panik. Fearon Teacher Aids, 1992.

## Materials Needed

- large brown grocery bag*
- various colored tissue paper strips
- glue
- scissors

## Tell the Class

If possible, bring a doll to class that is wearing a poncho.

Introduce this project to your students by saying, "The poncho is a very popular garment that is still worn in many places around the world, including Mexico. During siesta time (nap time) people sometimes tuck their arms under it and use it as a blanket."

## How to Make It

**For Teachers, Aides and Parent Volunteers**

**A.** Bring vividly colored photographs or illustrations from books that show Mexican people wearing ponchos. If possible, display a doll that is wearing one so that you can demonstrate how it easily slips over the head.

**B.** Cut various colors of tissue paper into 1½" x 17" (3.81 x 43.18 cm) strips.

## How to Make It

**For Students**

1. Open the bag so that it sits flat. Choose a corner seam and cut it from top to bottom.

2. Continue cutting all the way around the bottom of the bag. You should end up with one large flat piece of brown paper. If there is a logo showing, simply use the other side. (Young children may need an adult to do the cutting in these first two steps.)

3. Lay the paper horizontally and fold it in half.

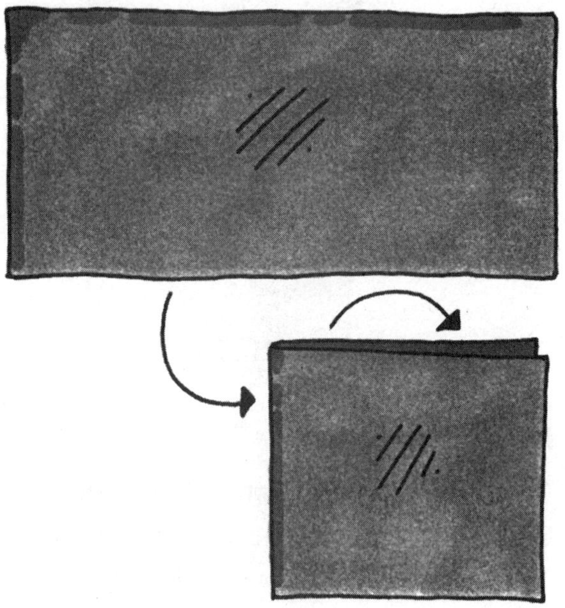

4. In the middle of the folded side, cut a large *V* shape. This will be the neck opening.

5. Glue the tissue paper strips horizontally across the front of the poncho.

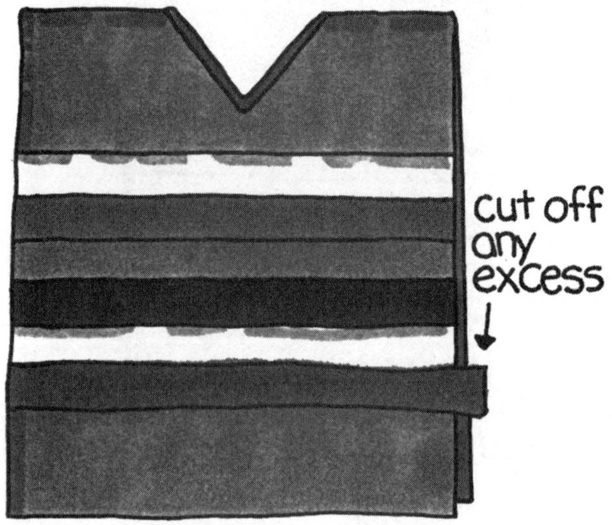


6. Cut 1" (2.54 cm) fringe along the bottom edges of the front and back.

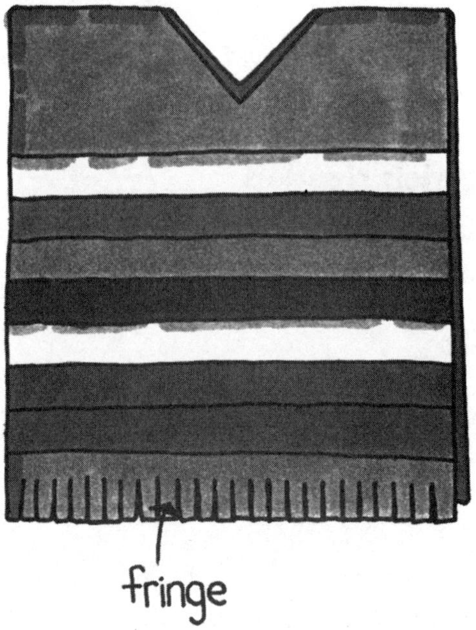


7. Wear your poncho at home. Pretend you are visiting Mexico.

# Musical Maracas

## ■ Perfect Timing

Make this craft when studying Mexico or reading:

- *How Music Came to the World: An Ancient Mexican Myth.* Hal Ober. Houghton Mifflin, 1994.
- *The Tree that Rains: The Flood Myth of the Huichol Indians of Mexico.* Emery Bernhard. Holiday House, 1994.
- *A Radio Man.* Arthur Dorros. HarperCollins Publishers, 1993.

## ■ Materials Needed

- small plastic spice bottle with cover (1.30 oz.)*
- craft stick*
- black, fine-tipped washable marker
- tape
- 10 popcorn kernels
- green, white and red construction paper scraps
- reproducible sombrero pattern
- crayons or washable markers
- glue
- scissors

## ■ Tell the Class

If possible, bring a pair of maracas to class.

"Maracas are a popular instrument in Mexico. Anyone can play one since all you need to do is shake them. Let's get going so that you can make a maraca of your very own!"

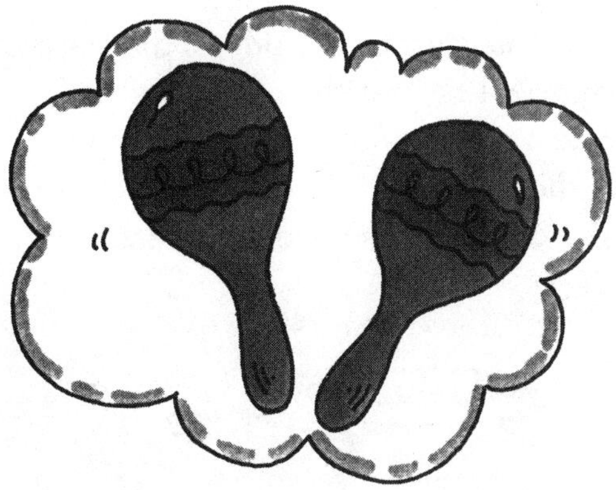

## ■ How to Make It

**For Teachers, Aides and Parent Volunteers**

**A.** Cut the green, white and red construction paper scraps into $\frac{3}{4}$" x $5\frac{3}{4}$" (1.91 x 14.61 cm) strips. Every child will need one of each color.

**B.** Photocopy a sombrero pattern for each student.

## ■ How to Make It

**For Students**

**1.** Remove the cover of the spice bottle and put the 10 popcorn kernels inside. Put the cover back on tightly.

2. Tape the craft stick to the side of the spice bottle. Position it so that the top of the stick is even with the top of the bottle. Wrap tape around the bottle and the stick several times. (Younger children will need assistance).

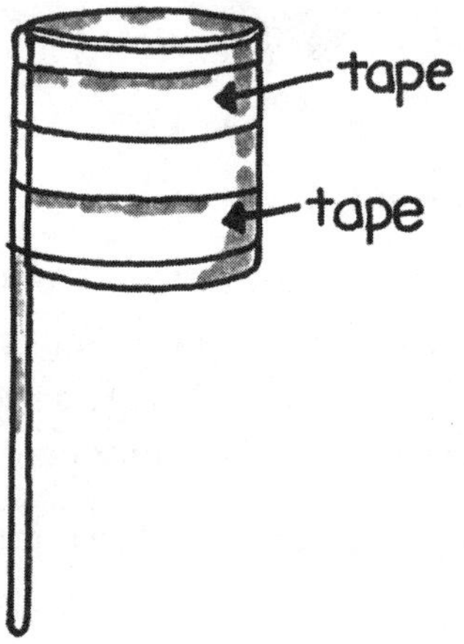


3. Use the black, fine-tipped washable marker to draw a zigzag pattern onto the red strip and a curly pattern onto the green strip as shown.

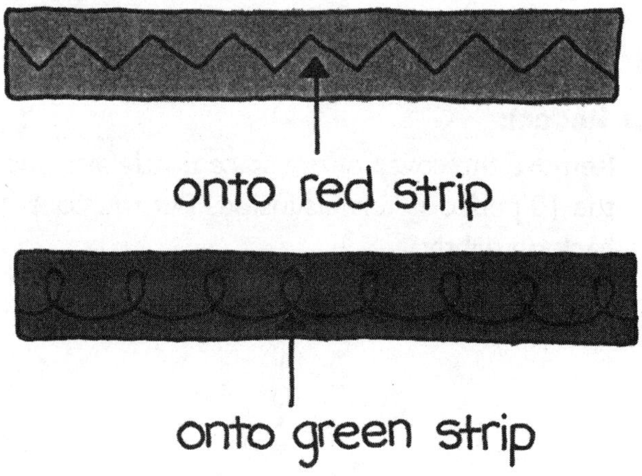


4. Glue the construction paper strips onto the bottle in this order: green at the bottom; white in the middle; red on the top. Tape the end of each strip to make it extra secure.

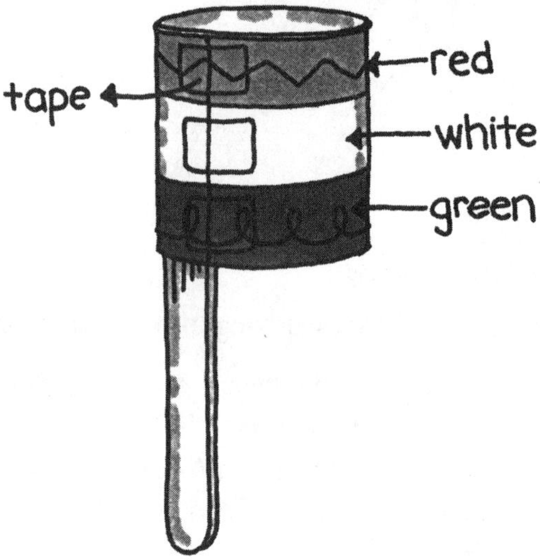


5. Color and then cut out the sombrero pattern. Tape it in place as shown.

6. Make up a short Mexican song, and shake your maraca as you sing it to a family member.

# Pretty Pottery

## ■ Perfect Timing

Make this craft when studying Mexico or reading:

- *Pancho's Piñata.* Stefan Czernecki and Timothy Rhodes. Hyperion Books for Children, 1992.
- *Too Many Tamales.* Gary Soto. Putnam, 1992.
- *The Twenty-Five Mixtex Cats.* Matthew Gollub. Tambourine Books, 1993.

## ■ Materials Needed

- cereal box (One can be shared by four students.)*
- liquid laundry detergent cap*
- modeling clay
- rice (a teaspoon)
- various colors of construction paper scraps
- masking tape
- green spray paint
- reproducible cactus pattern (page 59)
- crayons and washable markers
- glue
- scissors

## ■ Tell the Class

"The country of Mexico is well known for the beautiful pottery its people make.

Today you will design and make your own pot and put a pretend cactus in it."

## ■ How to Make It

**For Teachers, Aides and Parent Volunteers**

This craft takes two days to make. Do these steps on the first day.

**A.** Cut the front and back panels off of cereal boxes. Cut each panel in half as shown. Every student will need one piece.

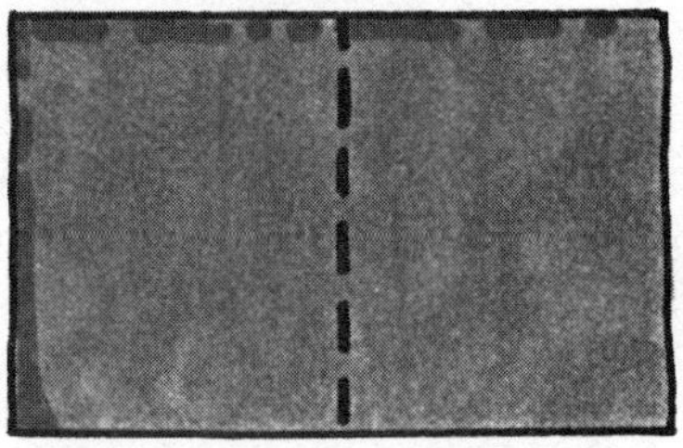

**B.** Photocopy a cactus pattern for each student. Have them cut out the cactus pattern on the dotted lines and glue the pattern onto the blank side of their cereal box panel. Tell them to let it dry, cut it out and bring it to you. Spray paint all the cactuses green on both sides.

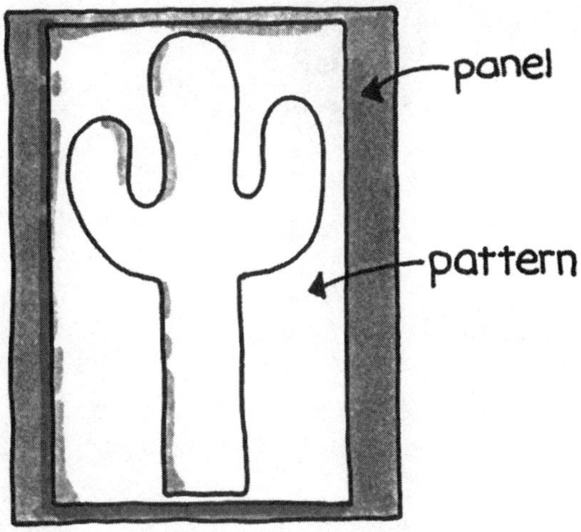

## How to Make It

### For Students

1. Cover the liquid detergent cap with 1" (2.54 cm) pieces of masking tape (overlapping the edges). Use a crayon to color over all the tape.

2. Decorate the pot by using markers and gluing on shapes cut from scraps of construction paper. Try to make a continuing pattern somewhere on the pot.

3. Randomly glue pieces of rice onto both sides of the cactus (to look like needles) as shown.

4. Put a small lump of clay onto the bottom of the cactus stem and place it firmly down into the pot.

# Cactus Pattern

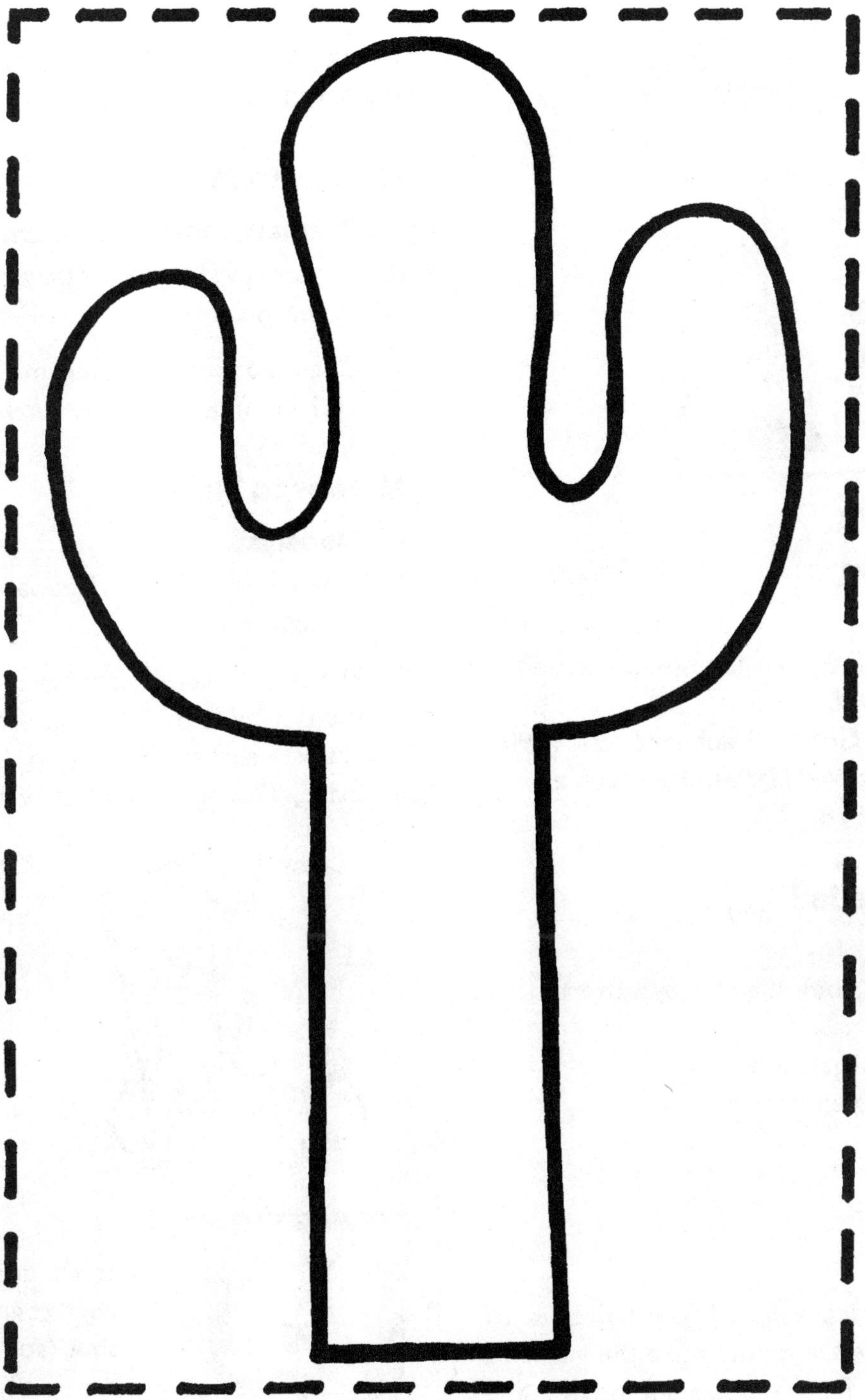

# Cute Cradleboard

## ■ Perfect Timing

Make this craft when studying Native Americans or reading:

- *The Legend of the Indian Paintbrush.* Tomie de Paola. Putnam, 1988.
- *Dream Wolf.* Paul Goble. Bradbury Press, 1990.
- *The Girl Who Loves Wild Horses.* Paul Goble. Bradbury Press, 1978.

## ■ Materials Needed

- 2 craft sticks*
- reproducible cradleboard and baby patterns (page 62)
- piece of yellow tissue paper
- crayons or washable markers
- tape
- scissors

## ■ Tell the Class

"Some Native Americans placed their babies in a cradleboard. This was something like the infant seats we have now. The baby was put into a cradleboard and leaned against a tree or hung on the side of a horse while traveling. It was also used as a cradle. Sometimes it was tied to a tree branch where it could swing gently in the breeze.

You will be making a cradleboard of your own. While you work, think of a name for your Native American baby."

## ■ How to Make It

**For Teachers, Aides and Parent Volunteers**

**A.** Photocopy the cradleboard and baby patterns for each student.

**B.** Cut yellow tissue paper into 4" x 4" (10.16 x 10.16 cm) pieces. Make one for each student.

## ■ How to Make It

**For Students**

1. Color one of the cradleboards and baby pattern and cut out.
2. Flip the cradleboard pattern over and fold on the dotted lines. Overlap the left panel so it almost reaches the fold on the right. Tape in place. (Younger students will need asssistance.)

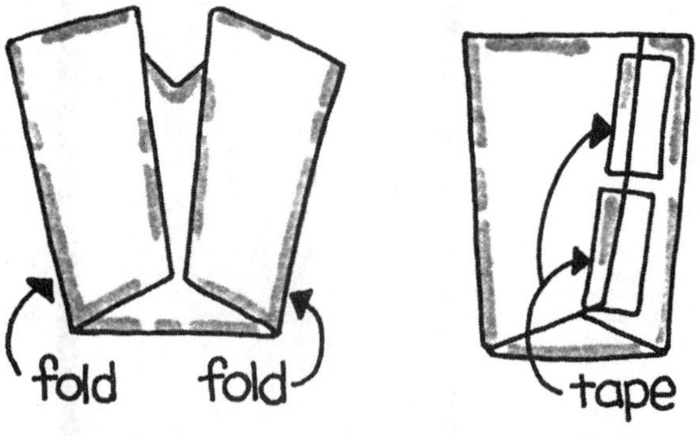


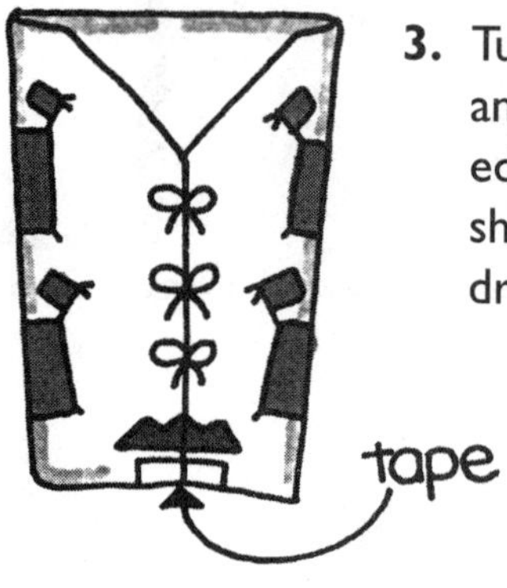


3. Turn the cradleboard over and squeeze the bottom edge together, and tape it shut (so the baby won't drop out).

4. Tape craft sticks to the back of the cradleboard so that the bottom of the sticks are even with the bottom edge of the cradleboard as shown. (Younger students will need assistance.)

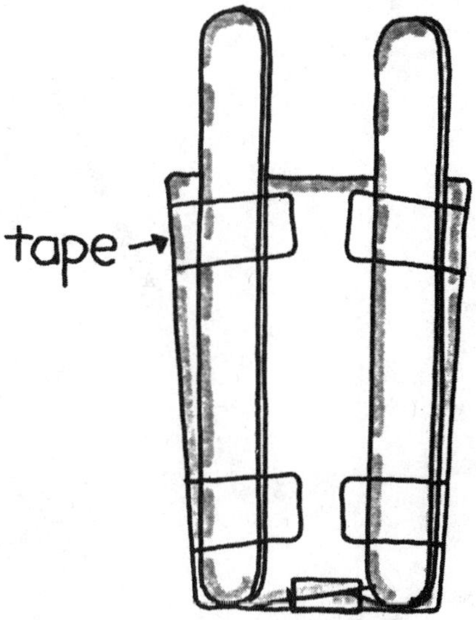


5. Fold the yellow tissue paper around the baby.

6. Place the wrapped baby into the cradleboard.

7. Take your cradleboard home and explain to family members how Native Americans used them.

# Cradleboard and Baby Patterns

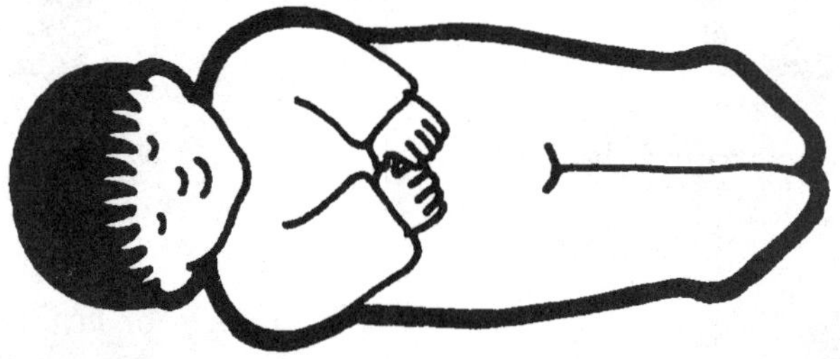

Design your own!

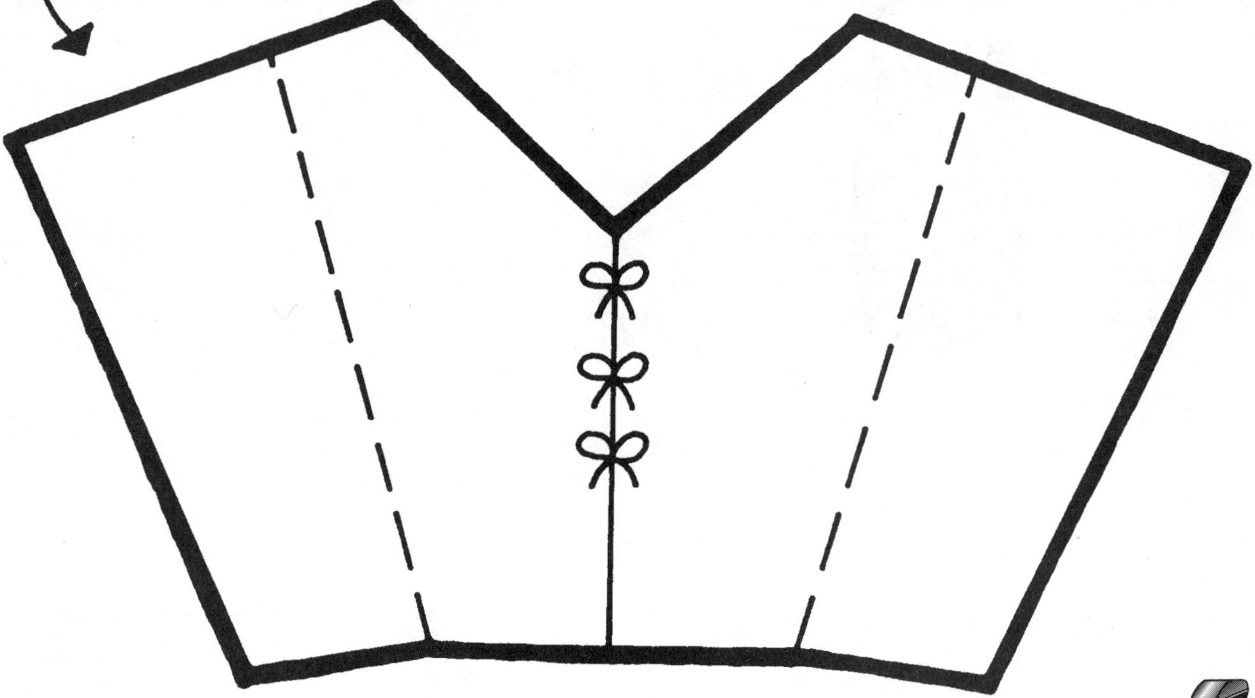

# Mini Hide Tanner

## ■ Perfect Timing

Make this craft when studying Native Americans or reading:

- *Knots on a Counting Rope*. Bill Martin, Jr., and John Archambault. Holt & Co., 1987.
- *Sky Dogs*. Jane Yolen. Harcourt Brace Jovanovich, 1990.
- *The Enchanted Caribou*. Elizabeth Cleaver. Atheneum Publishers, 1985.

## ■ Materials Needed

- 4 craft sticks*
- reproducible hide pattern (page 65)
- tan crayon
- brown fine-tip washable marker
- glue
- square of felt
- scissors

## ■ Tell the Class

"The Native Americans were very resourceful people. When they hunted an animal, they used the parts for many different things. They used the skin or *hide* of an animal to make clothing or as a canvas on which to draw pictures of important events. To do either of these things, they had to first scrape all the hair off of the skin and hang it on a wooden frame to dry.

Today we'll make a frame and place a pretend hide on it."

## ■ How to Make It

**For Teachers, Aides and Parent Volunteers**

**A.** Photocopy a hide pattern for each student.

**B.** Cut 5" x 5" (12.7 x 12.7 cm) pieces of tan felt. Every student will need one piece.

## ■ How to Make It

**For Students**

**1.** Position and glue the craft sticks into a square. (Younger students will need assistance.)

**2.** Use the brown fine-tip washable marker to draw a woodgrain pattern onto the sticks.

3. Color the hide pattern tan. Write your name on it. Cut out the pattern and glue the blank side onto the felt. Let it dry and cut it out.

4. Choose up to three Native American symbols. Color them tan. Cut them out and glue them onto the felt side of the hide.

5. Flip the hide over so the crayon side is showing. Put a small amount of glue in the spots shown.

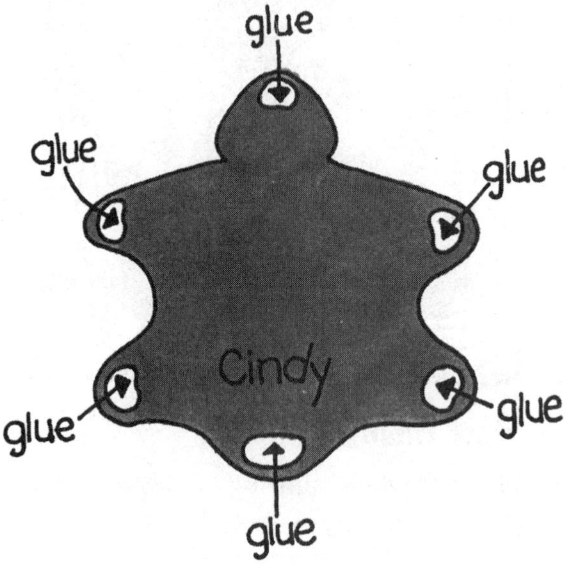


6. Carefully place the hide (felt side up) onto the craft stick frame and press down on all glued areas once. Let it dry.

7. Take it home and show your family.

# Hide Pattern

# Mysterious Mask

## Perfect Timing

Make this craft when studying Native Americans or reading:

- *Where the Buffalo Begin.* Olaf Baker. Warne, 1981. Puffin Books paperback available.
- *Hiawatha.* Henry Wadsworth Longfellow. Houghton Mifflin, 1920.
- *Corn Is Maize: The Gift of the Indians.* Aliki. Crowell, 1976.

## Materials Needed

- large brown grocery bag*
- various colors of construction paper scraps
- various colors and lengths of yarn scraps
- Native American Masks (page 68)
- washable markers
- glue
- scissors

## Tell the Class

"Some of the Native American tribes created masks. They used many different things to make the masks. Sometimes they used bones, deerskins and even corn husks. Native Americans used them for good luck and to communicate with their gods. Sometimes the masks were worn at a ceremony or to go along with dances and songs.

I'm going to give you a sheet that shows some samples of masks, and then I'd like each of you to create one of your own."

## How to Make It

### For Teachers, Aides and Parent Volunteers

**A.** Photocopy the Native American Masks page for each student.

**B.** Cut 7" (17.78 cm) off the top of all the bags (all the way around).

**C.** Have each student put the bag over their head so you can draw small circles where their eyes are. Then have them take if off so you can cut the eyeholes out. (Make them plenty big for safety reasons.)

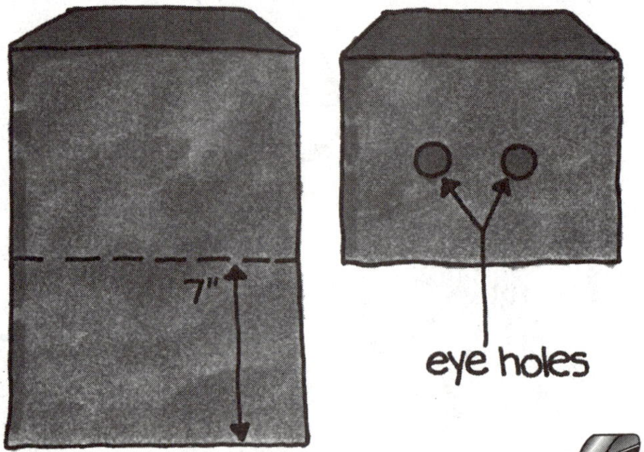

## How to Make It

### For Students

1. Look at the Native American Masks page or think up your own idea for a mask. Cut facial features out of construction paper scraps. Glue them onto the grocery bag mask.

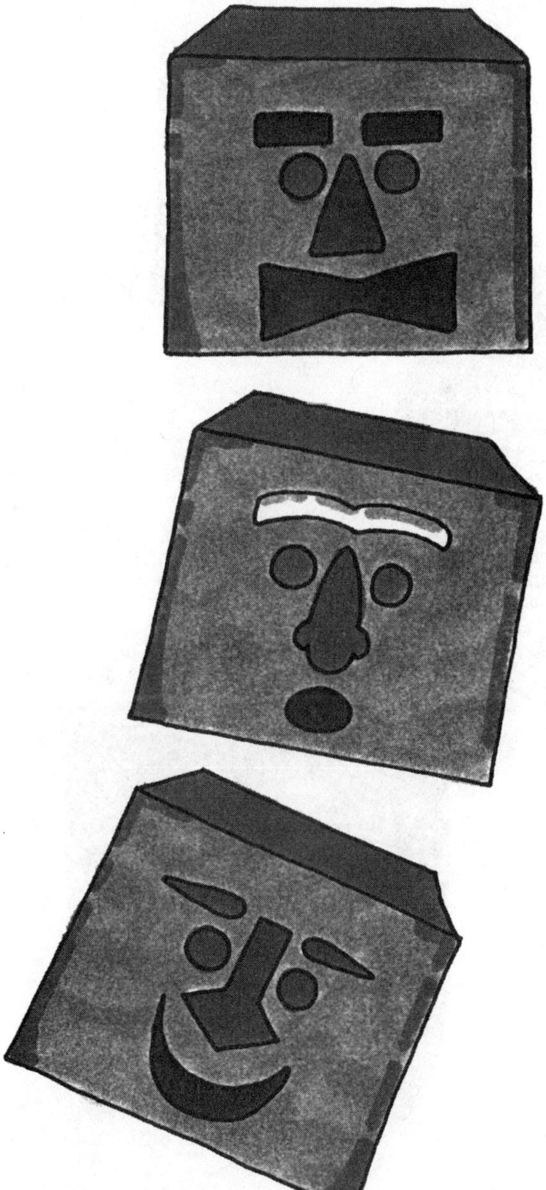

2. Decorate with yarn scraps. Use markers to add details. Put a "loop" of masking tape on your nose. Put your mask on and adjust it so you can see well out of the eyeholes. Then press the mask onto the masking tape on your nose to secure it in place. Take your mask home and model if for your family.

# Native American Masks

# Terrific Tepee

## Perfect Timing

Make this craft when studying Native Americans or reading:

- *Iktomi and the Buffalo Skull: A Plains Indian Story.* Paul Goble. Orchard Books, 1991.
- *Coyote Goes Hunting for Fire: A California Indian Myth.* Margery Bernstein and Janet Korbin. Scribner, 1974.
- *Arrow to the Sun: A Pueblo Indian Tale.* Gerald McDermott. Viking Press, 1974.

## Materials Needed

- round pizza cardboard (One can be shared by eight students.)*
- cereal box (One can be shared by fourteen students.)*
- orange and black construction paper scraps
- 1 uncooked spaghetti noodle
- black washable marker
- tape
- glue
- scissors

## Tell the Class

"Some Native Americans lived in tepees. Often the tepee was made from buffalo hides that were sewn together. Then it was placed over a cone-shaped frame. These Native Americans didn't stay long in one spot. They moved around a lot so they could hunt in different places. The tepee was the perfect home for them since it was so easy to pack up.

Let's make pretend tepees that really stand up!"

## How to Make It

**For Teachers, Aides and Parent Volunteers**

**A.** Cut the pizza cardboard into eight equally sized slices. On the curved edge of each slice, about ¾" (1.91 cm) from each side, cut two 1" (2.54 cm) slits as shown. Each student will need a slice.

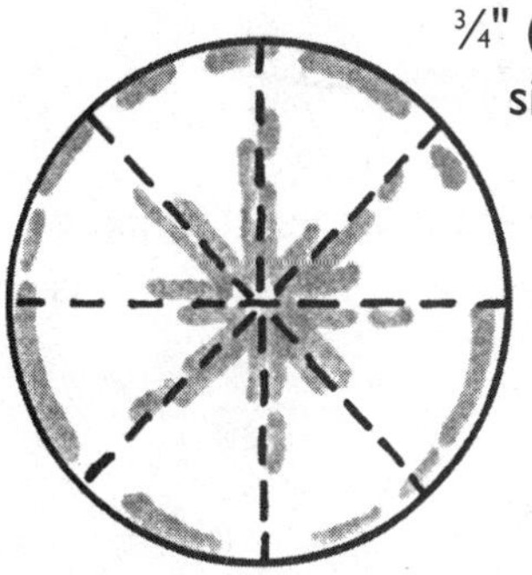

**B.** Cut 1" x 8" (2.54 x 20.32 cm) strips from the cereal boxes. Each child will need a strip.

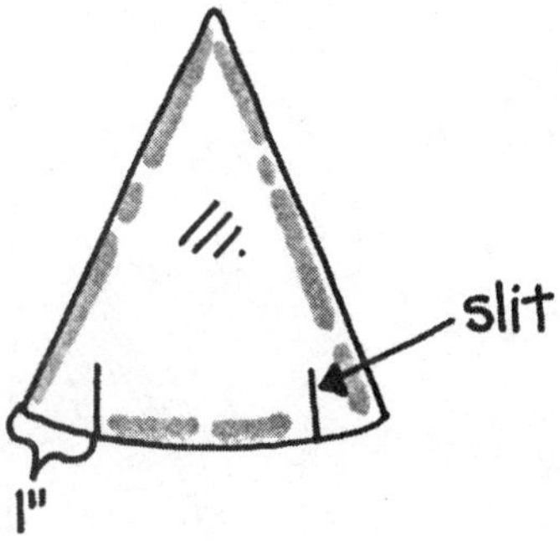


## How to Make it

**For Students**

**1.** Use the black washable marker to draw a line down the center of the cardboard slice.

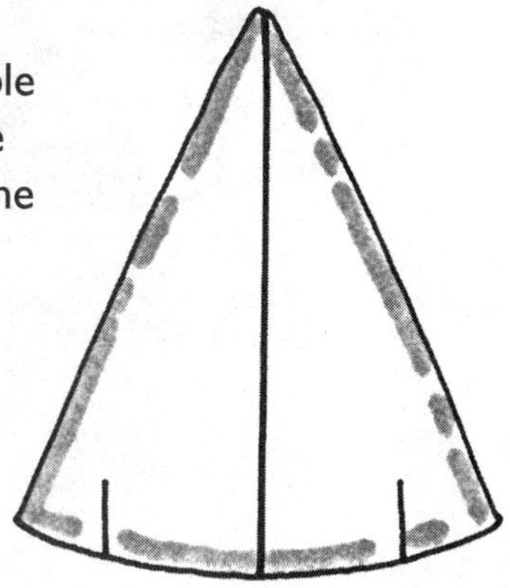

2. Cut a zigzag stripe out of orange construction paper and glue it near the bottom. (Younger students will need assistance.)

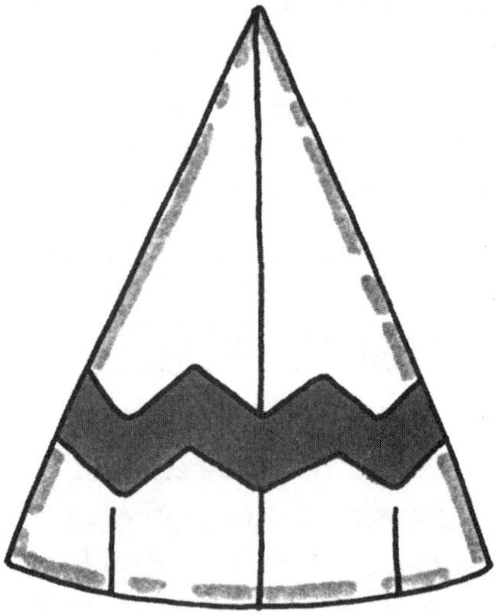

3. Cut a triangle from black construction paper and glue it onto the tepee as shown. This is the door.

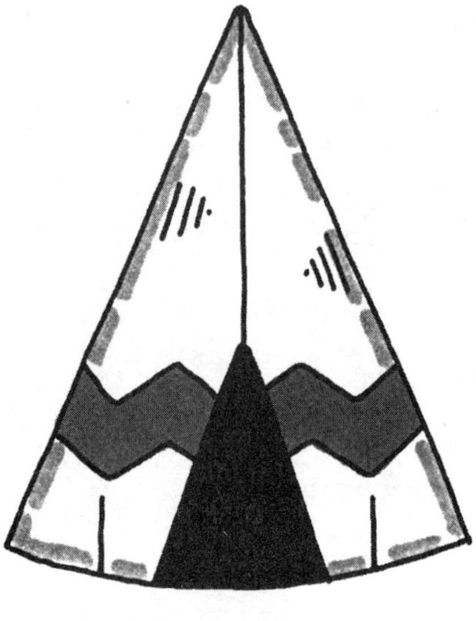

4. Break the spaghetti noodles into little pieces, and glue them above the door and onto the black line as shown. Cut little strips from the brown construction paper, and glue them behind the top of the tepee.

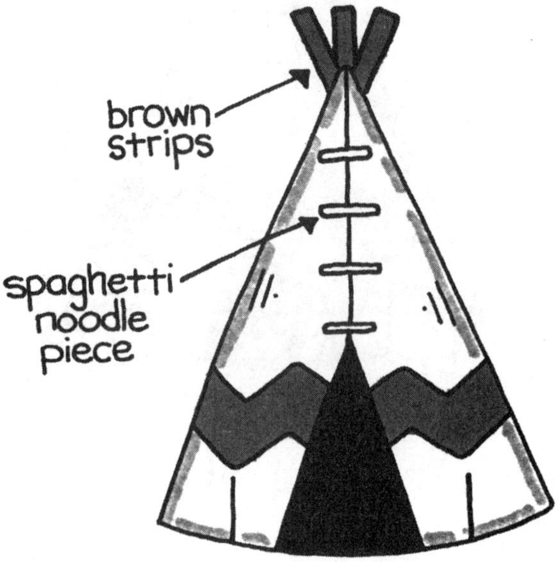


5. Take the cardboard strip and fold it in half. Then insert the ends into the slits to use as a stand.

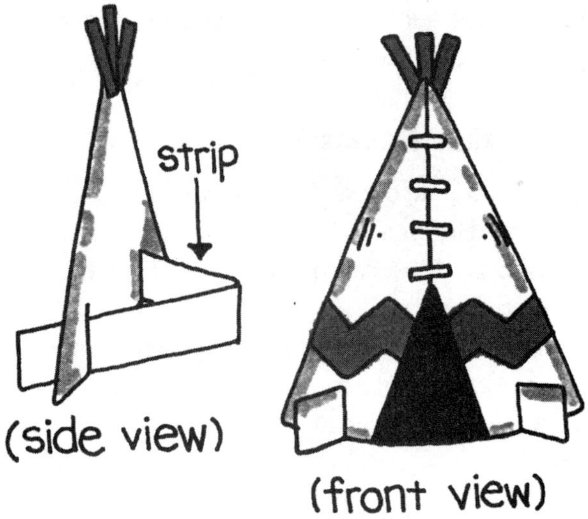


6. Take your tepee home and display it proudly on your dresser.

# Totally Awesome Totem Pole

## Perfect Timing

Make this craft when studying Native Americans or reading:

- *Whale in the Sky.* Ann Siberell. Dutton, 1982.
- *Fox Song.* Joseph Bruchac. Philomel Books, 1982.
- *The Land of Gray Wolf.* Thomas Locker. Dial Books, 1991.

## Materials Needed

- paper towel tube*
- various colors of construction paper
- reproducible face symbols patterns (page 73)
- crayons or washable markers
- glue
- scissors

## Tell the Class

"A totem pole is a wooden statue that is carved from a tree. Native Americans used them to tell stories of a tribe. The faces on totem poles usually represent animals, ancestors or spirits.

We're going to make totem poles today. When you're finished, think up a story about your totem pole and then tell a classmate."

## How to Make It

**For Teachers, Aides and Parent Volunteers**

**A.** Photocopy the face symbols patterns for each student.

**B.** Cut a variety of colored construction paper into 2¼" x 6" (5.72 x 15.24 cm) strips. Each student will need five strips.

## ■ How to Make It

### For Students

1. Cover the paper towel tube by gluing on the construction paper strips. First glue a strip on the top and bottom. Then fill the middle in with the remaining strips as shown.

2. Color the face symbols patterns. Cut them out. Glue the sun with the little face at the top of the totem pole. Glue the remaining faces on in any order you wish.

3. Take your totem pole home to use as an interesting decoration.

# Face Symbols Patterns

# Save 'n' Send

Dear Parent or Guardian:
We will be making crafts that use recyclable household items. Would you please help by sending the following circled items to school (cleaned and rinsed if necessary) with your child?

cardboard cereal boxes (flattened)
craft sticks (from frozen treats)
coffee cans with lids (1 lb. 10 oz.)
drinking straws (used and rinsed thoroughly)
frozen juice cans (12 oz. [354.9 ml])
frozen juice lids (12 oz. [354.9 ml])
grocery bags (large and brown)
liquid detergent caps
lunch bags (not soiled)
magazines (with lots of pictures of flowers)
newspapers
nondairy frozen topping lids (8" [20.32 cm] diameter)
paper towel tubes
round pizza cardboards
seed catalogs (with lots of pictures of flowers)
small plastic spice bottles with covers (1.30 oz.)
Styrofoam™ cups
Styrofoam™ trays
toilet tissue tubes
other: ______________________

If you have any questions, please feel free to call me. Thank you very much! I appreciate your cooperation!

Sincerely,

______________________ (teacher's name)    ______________________ (school's phone number)    ______________________ (date)

# Sufficiently Stocked

Dear Parent or Guardian:
Thank you very much for sending recyclable household items to school with your child to use for crafts. We now have plenty of the following circled items. You will no longer need to send them.

cardboard cereal boxes (flattened)
craft sticks (from frozen treats)
coffee cans with lids (1 lb. 10 oz.)
drinking straws (used and rinsed thoroughly)
frozen juice cans (12 oz. [354.9 ml])
frozen juice lids (12 oz. [354.9 ml])
grocery bags (large and brown)
liquid detergent caps
lunch bags (not soiled)
magazines (with lots of pictures of flowers)
newspapers
nondairy frozen topping lids (8" [20.32 cm] diameter)
paper towel tubes
round pizza cardboards
seed catalogs (with lots of pictures of flowers)
small plastic spice bottles with covers (1.30 oz.)
Styrofoam™ cups
Styrofoam™ trays
toilet tissue tubes
other: ______________________

If you have any questions, please feel free to call me. Thank you very much! I appreciate your cooperation!

Sincerely,

______________________ (teacher's name)    ______________________ (school's phone number)    ______________________ (date)

# I Choose to Reuse!

I have learned many interesting things while making multicultural crafts. To make these crafts, I used recyclable household items. It was lots of fun! I will try to always **Choose to Reuse** and make our world a cleaner place!

______________________________________________
(student's name)

______________________________ ______________
(teacher's name) (date)

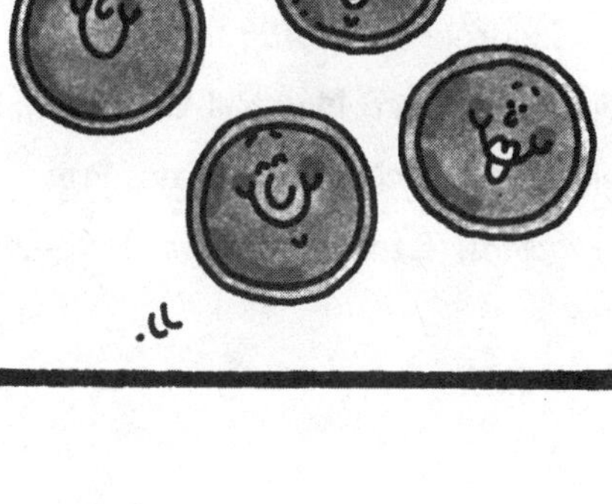

# Resources


*Adventures in Art: Art and Craft Experiences for 7-14 Year-Olds.* Susan Milord. Williamson Publishing, 1990.

*A Family in Colombia.* Peter Otto Jacobsen and Preben Sejer Kristensen. The Bookwright Press, 1986.

*America's Fascinating Indian Heritage.* The Reader's Digest Association, 1978.

*Ashanti to Zulu: African Traditions.* Margaret Musgrove. Dial Press, 1976.

*Brazil.* Evelyn Bender. Chelsea House Publishers, 1990.

*Brazil.* Karen Jacobsen. Childrens Press, 1989.

*Brazil.* Wilbur and Susanna Cross. Childrens Press, 1984.

*The Africans Knew.* Tillie S. Pine and Joseph Levine. McGraw-Hill Book Company, 1967.

*The Cherokee.* Barbara A. McCall. Rourke Publications, 1990.

*The Children of China.* Matti A. Pitkanen with Reijo Harkonen. Carolrhoda Books, 1990.

*China.* Karen Jacobsen. Childrens Press, 1990.

*The Chinese Knew.* Tillie S. Pine and Joseph Levine. McGraw-Hill Book Company, 1958.

*Count Your Way Through Korea.* Jim Haskins. Carolrhoda Books, Inc., 1989.

*Early Japan.* Jonathan Norton Leonard. Time-Life Books, 1968.

*Family Fun Magazine.* October Issue, 1994.

*The First Americans.* Robert Claiborne. Time-Life Books, 1973.

*The Great Wall of China.* Leonard Everett Fisher. Macmillan, 1986.

*Guatemala—Children of the World.* Ronald Cummins. Gareth Stevens Children's Books, 1990.

*Guatemala.* Marlene Targ Brill and Harry R. Targ. Childrens Press, 1993.

*India.* Srinivasan. Marshall Cavendish, 1990.

*India.* Sylvia McNair. Childrens Press, 1990.

*The Indians.* Benjamin Capps. Time-Life Books, 1976.

*Indians of the Arctic and Subarctic.* Paula Younkin. Facts on File, 1992.

*India: The Land and Its People.* Natasha Talyarkhan. Silver Burdett Co., 1975.

*International Picture Library—Children Around the World.* Lynda Snowdon, Dillon Press Inc., 1986.

*The Inuit.* Elizabeth Hahn. Rourke Publications, 1990.

*Italy.* Conrad R. Stein. Childrens Press, 1984.

*Italy.* Patricia Borlenghi and Rachel Wright. Franklin Watts, 1993.

*Italy: The Land and Its People.* Michael Leech. Silver Burdett Co., 1974.

*Japan.* Peter Spry-Leverton, Peter Kornicki. Facts on File, 1987.

*Japan.* Rex Shelley. Marshall Cavendish, 1990.

*Journey Through Mexico.* Barbara Bulmer-Thomas. Troll Associates, 1991.

*Kenya.* Conrad R. Stein. Childrens Press, 1985.

*Korea.* Jill Dubois. Marshall Cavendish, 1994.

*Korea.* Karen Jacobsen. Childrens Press, 1989.

*Mexico.* Yoshiyuki Ikahara. Gareth Stevens Publishing, 1987.

*Mexico.* Karen Jacobsen. Childrens Press, 1982.

*North American Indian Arts.* Andrew Hunter and White Ford. Golden Press, 1970.

*Nicaragua.* Ronald Cummins. Gareth Stevens Children's Books, 1990.

*Panama.* Anna Maria Vazquez. Childrens Press, 1991.

*The Piñata Maker=El Piñatero.* George Ancona. Harcourt Brace, 1994.

*South Africa.* Barbara Radcliffe Rogers. Gareth Stevens Children's Books, 1991.

*They Put on Masks.* Byrd Baylor. Scribner, 1974.

*This Place Is Crowded: Japan.* Vicki Cobb. Walker, 1992.